PRACTICE
MAKES
PERFECT™

French
Nouns and
Their Genders
Up Close

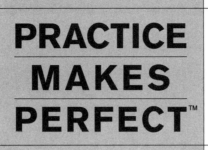

**PRACTICE
MAKES
PERFECT**™

French
Nouns and
Their Genders
Up Close

Annie Heminway

New York   Chicago   San Francisco   Lisbon   London   Madrid   Mexico City
Milan   New Delhi   San Juan   Seoul   Singapore   Sydney   Toronto

Contents

Preface

POLONIUS: « Que lisez-vous là, monseigneur? »
HAMLET: « Des mots, des mots, des mots! »

—William Shakespeare, *Hamlet*, Act II, scene 2

This is not an ordinary book about words. The dismissive irony in Hamlet's response is impressive, but we know that a word can kill, cause profound mental distress, destroy a love, demolish a career, undermine a friendship, and even start a war. A carefully chosen word, **le mot juste**, as we say in French, can make the difference between triumph and tragedy. In English, all we need to know is the word itself. In French, however, knowing just the word is not enough; if we want to avoid embarrassment, even danger, we must know the word's gender, which is either feminine or masculine. Everybody knows what a **mousse** is, but woe to the learner who, unaware of the correct gender (feminine), tells his French interlocutor about *le* **mousse** (masculine) that he just made, for that word means "cabin boy."

Learning the correct gender is not always easy, but this book, which includes many rules, tips, ideas, and suggestions, will be your trusty guide through the labyrinths of French genders. After you master the rules, you will be prepared to approach the mystery of gender, but you will also have to proceed as a poet, using your ear as well as your intuition, to identify the true being of a particular word in the melody of a French phrase.

The magnificent, mysterious, enchanting world of French genders will open the door to the fascinating history of the French language. Without having to consult dusty volumes, you will discover that the modern French gender system came to us via numerous circuitous and dizzying paths, all the way from the dawn of time, when humans categorized all beings as either animate or inanimate, progressing, so to speak, to Latin and culminating in contemporary usage.

Having lost the Latin neuter gender, French retained the feminine-masculine dichotomy. This is an important fact. Please don't be fooled by those (this group includes some linguists and many pessimists) who claim that French genders are totally random, disconnected from reality, and almost impossible to learn. Going beyond the rules spelled out in this book, you will always be able to tap into your knowledge of history, mythology, and psychology. For example, in the light of the moon's significance in certain mythologies, you will not be surprised by its feminine gender in French. The German poet Heinrich Heine always yearned for the "natural" femininity of the word *moon*, finding the masculine gender of the German word for the moon (*der Mond*) quite inappropriate.

Delving further into the past, you will find that certain archetypal words, such as *source* and *earth*, have kept that ancient gender (feminine) in French. The great French philosopher Gaston Bachelard loved to ponder the rich male-female dialectics of *animus*, which in Latin means "rational mind," and *anima*, which means "soul." When you think of the soul's qualities, you will understand why French has kept the Latin feminine gender in one of its most beautiful and expressive words: **âme**.

In 1966, Jean-Luc Godard, a key director of French New Wave cinema, released his film ***Masculin, féminin***. A movie about grammar? No, rather a movie about young people, sex, gender, and politics in France in the late 1960s. ***Masculin, féminin*** has become a cult film for English-speaking viewers, as there is no aspect of learning a foreign language that presents more difficulties than the question of gender. Why is that?

Most languages have two types of gender: natural and grammatical. Natural gender is based on biology: human beings and animals that are male are masculine; those that are female are feminine. Everything else is neuter. This is in contrast to grammatical gender, which is simply a property of the noun. Modern English is rare in that it is one of the few widely spoken languages without grammatical gender.

The idea of grammatical gender may seem straightforward—every noun is masculine or feminine and that is that. However, it is not always that simple. For example, there are nouns that are masculine in the singular but become feminine in the plural, such as **délice** (*delight*). There are nouns that can be masculine or feminine with the same meaning, such as **oasis** (*oasis*). More confusing are those that can be masculine or feminine but with a different meaning. Consider the following example: **J'ai payé une livre pour ce livre** (*I paid one pound sterling for this book*). Or this: **Le marin lève la voile. Puis il lève le voile de dentelle de la jeune femme** (*The sailor raises the sail. Then he raises the young woman's lace veil*). Or: **J'ai trouvé de belles fleurs dans le vase, pas dans la vase** (*I found beautiful flowers in the vase, not in the slime*). And these subtleties sometimes may lead to diplomatic incidents such as: **Il ne sera pas possible de trouver une poste dans cette région** (*It won't be possible to find a post office in this area*). But the official really meant: **Il ne sera pas possible de trouver un poste dans cette region** (*It won't be possible to find a position in this area*).

It is important to remember that grammatical gender is not always permanent, either, with some nouns changing gender over time. And then there are the new words. Just who decides what gender to give a word like *Bluetooth*, for example? **La dent** (*tooth*) is feminine, but **Bluetooth** is masculine.

This book is meant to be a comprehensive overview to students who may be unaccustomed to the uses and pitfalls of grammatical gender. It is meant to be used as a guide, with chapters devoted to individual topics. Remember, sometimes even native French speakers are unsure and have to look things up! And who knows, perhaps a future film entitled *Masculin, féminin* may actually be about grammar and be based on our new adventure with gender.

The magic and romance of French gender

Basic endings and other cases

As you already know, there are two genders in French: masculine and feminine, preceded by the definite article **le**, **la** or the indefinite article **un**, **une**. Since the purpose of this book is to forge a reliable method of identifying and learning French genders, we will learn the fundamental rules governing genders, starting with masculine nouns and then moving on the feminine nouns. Along with the rules, we will identify their exceptions. Indeed, exceptions to grammatical rules can be annoying, but this is a "flaw" of all natural languages. (Only constructed languages, such as Esperanto, contain rules without exceptions.)

While you may be tempted to say that French gender can sometimes be arbitrary, you do have some name endings to rely on. Memorization is crucial. Every new word must be learned in conjunction with its gender. This knowledge, as you will find out, quickly becomes tacit, internalized. After some practice, you will be able to identify the gender of a word by relying on your intuition, without even having to think in terms of rules and exceptions.

In your mind, each word will become like a short musical phrase. You won't have to think which key, major or minor, the musical phrase is in. You will simply know. When you study music, you learn scales. In French: **do, ré, mi, fa, sol, la, si, do**. Learning endings is similar. **Le train**, **le bateau**, and **le vin** will come on your masculine scale, whereas **la beauté**, **la nature**, and **la culture** will register on your feminine scale. French is all about sounds. Gustave Flaubert used to isolate himself and shout his novels aloud in his **gueuloir**—more or less his screaming room—to make sure the words flowed beautifully. Think of endings as musical notes on a score.

In this chapter, you will learn how to connect a noun to its gender marker by studying the main endings of masculine nouns. Feminine nouns will follow. For example, nouns ending in a consonant or in any vowel but **e** tend to be masculine:

le bijou	*jewel*	**le gaz**	*gas*	**le sofa**	*sofa*
le cacao	*cocoa*	**le lieu**	*place*	**le tact**	*tact*
le carnaval	*carnival*	**le nez**	*nose*	**le zébu**	*zebu*
le gala	*gala*				

As we proceed, remember to focus on the endings and, at the same time, to memorize any exceptions that may crop up.

Basic masculine noun endings

The following endings tend to be masculine.

-age, -ige, -ège, -oge, -uge

l'éloge	praise	le prodige	prodigy, feat
le fromage	cheese	le refuge	refuge
le mariage	marriage	le sortilège	spell

Stéphane Audeguy a écrit un livre merveilleux, *Le petit éloge de la douceur*.	Stéphane Audeguy wrote a wonderful book, In **Praise** of Sweetness.
Les alpinistes ont dormi dans **un refuge**.	*The climbers slept in **a refuge**.*
Félicie a offert un fauteuil art déco à sa cousine comme cadeau de **mariage**.	*Félicie gave her cousin an Art Deco armchair as a **wedding** gift.*

However, there are a few exceptions:

la cage	cage	la Norvège	Norway
l'horloge	clock	la page	page
l'image	image	la plage	beach
la loge	dressing room/lodge	la rage	rage, fury, rabies
la luge	luge	la tige	stem
la nage	swimming		

Il manque **la** dernière **page** du livre.	***The** last **page** of the book is missing.*
Nous avons félicité **la diva** dans **sa loge**.	*We congratulated **the diva** in **her dressing room**.*

-ail, -euil

l'épouvantail	scarecrow	le seuil	doorstep, threshold
le fauteuil	armchair	le travail	work
le recueil	collection, anthology	le vitrail	stained-glass window

Henri a mis **un épouvantail** dans son jardin.	*Henri has placed **a scarecrow** in his garden.*
Zoé lit **un recueil** de poèmes dans **son fauteuil**.	*Zoé is reading **a poetry book** in **her armchair**.*

-ain

le bain	*bath, swim*		**le pain**	*bread*
le grain	*grain*		**le terrain**	*ground, land*
le lendemain	*following day*		**le train**	*train*

There is one exception: **la main** (*hand*).

Samuel est arrivé le 3 mars et il est reparti **le lendemain**.

*Samuel arrived on March 3rd and left **the following day**.*

Va acheter **du pain** avant de prendre **ton bain**.

*Go buy **some bread** before taking **a bath**.*

-al

le cheval	*horse*		**le mal**	*harm, pain, evil*
le festival	*festival*		**le récital**	*recital*
le journal	*newspaper*		**le signal**	*signal*

Armelle a lu dans **le journal** qu'il y aurait **un récital** de musique baroque **au festival** de La Rochelle.

*Armelle read in **the paper** that there would be **a recital** of baroque music **at the** La Rochelle **festival**.*

Le cheval d'Henri IV était-il vraiment blanc?

*Was Henri IV's **horse** really white?*

-ament, -ement

le branchement	*connection*		**le médicament**	*medicine/medication*
le département	*department*		**le réchauffement**	*warming*
le jugement	*judgment/sentence*		**le testament**	*testament*

Ce médicament est recommandé pour l'hypertension.

***This drug** is recommended for high blood pressure.*

Vu les problèmes dans la famille, il n'a pas encore fait **son testament**.

*Given the family problems, he has not yet made out **his will**.*

-ard

le canard	*duck*		**le regard**	*look/gaze*
le guépard	*cheetah*		**le renard**	*fox*
le placard	*cupboard*		**le vieillard**	*old man*

Une famille de **canards** habite sur l'étang.

*A family of **ducks** lives on the pond.*

Son regard se posa sur elle.

***His eyes** came to rest on her.*

Some words ending in -**ard** may have a pejorative connotation, such as:

le bâtard	*bastard, illegitimate child*	**le fêtard**	*reveler*
le chauffard	*reckless driver*	**le vantard**	*boaster*
le clochard	*bum*		

-eau, -ou

le bateau	*boat*	**le chameau**	*camel*
le bijou	*jewel*	**le château**	*castle*
le cerveau	*brain*	**le chou**	*cabbage*

Here are two exceptions: **la peau** (*skin*), **l'eau** (*water*).

Patrick était **le cerveau** de l'affaire.	*Patrick was **the brains** behind the job.*
On lui a volé tous **ses bijoux**.	*All of **her jewelery** was stolen.*

English and French share many nouns of Latin origin. It will come in handy to compare and deduce the meaning of words. For instance, these two particular exceptions are interesting, for they have retained the gender of their Latin ancestors: *pellis* (*skin*) and *aqua* (*water*).

-el

l'appel	*call*	**le matériel**	*equipment, material*
le caramel	*caramel*	**le sel**	*salt*
le logiciel	*software*		

Ce logiciel vous permettra de créer un site web.	*This software will help you create a website.*
Passe-moi **le sel**, s'il te plaît.	*Pass me **the salt**, please.*

-ent, -ant

l'argent	*money*	**le restaurant**	*restaurant*
le chant	*singing, song*	**le talent**	*talent*
le diamant	*diamond*	**le vent**	*wind*

Here is one exception: **la dent** (*tooth*). And more Latin: *dens* (*tooth*) is feminine.

Églantine a emprunté de **l'argent** à sa mère.	*Églantine borrowed **money** from her mother.*
Puis elle s'est offert une bague **en diamant**.	*Then she treated herself to **a diamond** ring.*

-er

le boulanger	*baker*	**le fer**	*iron*
le danger	*danger*	**le passager**	*passenger*
le déjeuner	*lunch*	**le verger**	*orchard*

Ils ne produisent que des poires Williams dans **ce verger**.

Si on prenait **du pain perdu** au petit déjeuner?

*They only produce Williams pears in **this orchard**.*

*What about having **some French toast** for breakfast?*

-ier/yer

le calendrier	*calendar*	**le loyer**	*rent*
le clavier	*keyboard*	**le tablier**	*apron*
le fichier	*file*	**le voilier**	*sailboat*

Adèle n'a pas pu ouvrir **ton fichier**.

Le loyer est-il cher pour ce studio?

*Adèle could not open **your file**.*

*Is **the rent** expensive for this studio?*

-at, -et, -t

l'alphabet	*alphabet*	**le débat**	*debate*
le billet	*ticket*	**le lit**	*bed*
le circuit	*circuit, tour*	**le perroquet**	*parrot*

Nous regarderons **le débat** à la télé ce soir.

Ils dorment dans **un lit** à baldaquin.

*We'll watch **the debate** on TV tonight.*

*They sleep in **a** four-poster **bed**.*

Here are quite a few important exceptions:

la dot	*dowry*	**la nuit**	*night*
la forêt	*forest*	**la part**	*share*
la mort	*death*	**la plupart**	*most people/things*

There were no sneakers in ancient Rome, of course. The Latin word for *forest*, *silva*, although feminine, does not even resemble the French noun; however, it appears in words such as **sylviculture** (*forestry*). But look at the Latin roots of the other feminine words: *nox* (*night*), *mors* (*death*), *pars* (*part, share*), and *dos* (*dowry*).

La nuit, tous les chats sont gris.

De nombreuses espèces de perroquets se trouvent dans **la forêt** tropicale de l'île Maurice.

*Everyone looks the same **in the dark**.*

*Many species of parrot are to be found in **the** tropical **forest** of Mauritius Island.*

-eur

Nouns ending in **-eur** include names of professions as well as words denoting certain tools and machines.

l'aspirateur	*vacuum cleaner*	le compositeur	*composer*
le climatiseur	*air-conditioner*	l'ordinateur	*computer*
le cœur	*heart*	le réfrigérateur	*refrigerator*

Léa, tu devrais passer **l'aspirateur** dans le salon.   *Léa, you should **vacuum** the living room.*

Paul-Henri a **un cœur** de pierre.   *Paul-Henri has **a heart** of stone.*

Don't be intimidated by the references to Latin. No one expects a budding—or even competent—Francophone to become a Latinist. However, Latin is not only the direct ancestor of French but also a living presence. When a French-speaking person dips into the vast ocean of Latin vocabulary to create a handy neologism, he or she, as scholars have written, is not borrowing from a foreign language.

While English is a bit removed from Latin, let us not forget the Norman Conquest (1066), which imposed Norman French on England for more than three centuries. English was not accepted in the courts until 1386, becoming the fully accepted idiom only around 1400. As a result, modern English retains an enormous Latin vocabulary, acquired via Norman French. In fact, English is probably more French than any other non-Romance language, and English speakers use French in everyday life without even knowing it. For example, while *love* is a Germanic word, its adjective, *amorous,* is French. We are so used to our Romance vocabulary that we don't even notice our natural bilingualism when we alternate, depending on the context, between *friendly* (Germanic) and *amicable* (French). There are thousands of such examples—no surprise, since around 30 percent of our vocabulary is French. These affinities and similarities between English and French are good news for the learner.

In another example, we are all familiar with an elegant French word for *software*: **logiciel**. But the word for *gameware*, **ludiciel**, is equally elegant. Why **ludiciel**, you might wonder, since the word for game is **jeu**? But the Latin word for game is *ludus*, and the neologism sounds quite native to a French ear. Another interesting Latin-derived word is the French word for *computer*, **ordinateur**. It comes from the Latin *ordinator*, which means not only, literally, *the one who puts things in order*, but is also a synonym for *God!*

-ien

le bien	good	l'italien	Italian
le chien	dog	le lien	link, tie
l'entretien	interview, upkeep, maintenance	le végétarien	vegetarian

Ludovic ne sait pas discerner **le bien** du mal.

*Ludovic is not able to tell **good** from evil.*

L'entretien de ces jardins coûte une fortune.

***The maintenance** of these gardens costs a fortune.*

-illon

le bouillon	broth, bubble	le grillon	cricket
le brouillon	first draft, outline	le papillon	butterfly
l'échantillon	sample	le tourbillon	whirlwind, swirl

Voudriez-vous **un échantillon** de ce tissu en lin?

*Would you like **a sample** of this linen fabric?*

La bibliothèque Mitterrand a organisé une exposition sur **les brouillons** des plus grands écrivains.

*The Mitterrand Library organized an exhibit on the greatest writers' **drafts**.*

-in

le chagrin	grief	le moulin	mill
le dessin	drawing, design	le vin	wine
le jardin	garden		

One exception is **la fin** (*end*).

Théo a fait **un** joli **dessin** dans **le jardin**.

*Théo did **a** nice **drawing** in **the garden**.*

Le meunier est mort de **chagrin** dans **son moulin**.

*The miller died of **sorrow** in **his mill**.*

-is

le compromis	compromise	le fouillis	mess, jumble
le croquis	sketch	le taudis	slum
le devis	estimate	le tennis	tennis

There are two exceptions: **la souris** (*mouse*) and **la vis** (*screw*).

Pourriez-vous nous donner **un devis** pour les réparations?	*Could you give us **an estimate** for the repairs?*
Quel fouillis! Je ne retrouve même plus **la souris** de mon ordinateur!	***What a mess!** I can't even find **my** computer **mouse**!*

-isme

l'égoïsme	selfishness	le romantisme	romanticism
l'héroïsme	heroism	le séisme	earthquake
l'optimisme	optimism	le socialisme	socialism

Le séisme a fait de nombreuses victimes.	***The earthquake** killed many people.*
L'héroïsme de la population était inouï.	***The heroism** of the people was unbelievable.*

-oir, -oin

le besoin	need	le miroir	mirror
le coin	corner, part	le témoin	witness
le couloir	hallway	le trottoir	sidewalk

Sabrine a **besoin** d'**un** nouveau **miroir**.	*Sabrine **needs a** new **mirror**.*
Appelez **le témoin**!	*Call **the witness**!*

-on, -om

le cornichon	gherkin	le salon	living room
le nom	name	le torchon	dish towel
le prénom	first name	le violon	violin

Here are a few exceptions:

la boisson	beverage	la leçon	lesson
la chanson	song	la livraison	delivery
la cloison	partition	la rançon	ransom
la cuisson	cooking	la trahison	betrayal
la façon	manner		

Passe-moi **le torchon** jaune!	*Hand me **the** yellow **dish towel**!*
Quelle est l'origine de **ce prénom**?— Maylis? Je crois que c'est breton.	*What is the origin of **this first name**?— Maylis? I think it is Breton.*

Bear in mind that the -**on** ending often indicates Latin ancestry and that many feminine Latin words ending with -**tio** acquired -**tion** endings, which are also feminine in French. Thus the Latin *natio* became **nation**. In the same vein, **chanson** comes from *cantio* and **leçon** from *lectio*. It is safe to say that you have to be extra careful with -**on** words. For example, **son** (*sound*) retains the masculine gender of *sonus*, its Latin ancestor, whereas words like **nation** are feminine. It might be helpful to treat -**tion** as a separate ending, which always indicates a feminine word.

-phone

Nouns ending with -**phone** are masculine, often referring to machines and instruments connected to sound. This is a bit funny, because this ending stems from the Greek word for voice, *phōnē*, which is feminine, just as the French word **voix**, which comes from the equally feminine Latin *vox*. Yes, Greek, too, lurks behind the scenes, but there is no need for panic. In French, we get to enjoy the lexical opulence of the two classical languages without having to learn their respective grammars. That is a good thing, of course, since French grammar, as we know, is enough of a challenge.

le magnétophone	*tape recorder*	**le saxophone**	*saxophone*
le mégaphone	*megaphone*	**le téléphone**	*telephone*
le microphone	*microphone*	**le xylophone**	*xylophone*

Leur téléphone est en dérangement.
Guillaume joue **du saxophone** dans un club le jeudi soir.

Their phone is out of order.
Guillaume plays the saxophone in a club on Thursday nights.

-scope

Nouns ending in -**scope** refer to optical instruments and related things, which makes sense, because the suffix comes from the Greek verb *skopeo*, which means *I look* and *I spy on someone*.

l'horoscope	*horoscope*	**le microscope**	*microscope*
le kaléidoscope	*kaleidoscope*	**le téléscope**	*telescope*
le magnétoscope	*videotape recorder*	**le trombinoscope**	*group photo*

Isabeau lit **son horoscope** tous les matins dans le journal.
Nous avons observé Vénus grâce **au téléscope** d'Alix.

Isabeau reads her horoscope every morning in the paper.
We looked at Venus thanks to Alix's telescope.

As you have seen, there is some method in the madness of genders. True, there is no set of rules, free of exceptions, that one could memorize and thereby master French genders. If that were true, there would be no need for this book! However, by memorizing the principal ending types, you will make great strides toward mastery. You might even decide that incomplete mastery may be OK, because it leaves room for mystery.

Other masculine endings

You thought you were done with masculine endings? Not so fast. There are other interesting cases.

-a

Nouns ending with -a are usually masculine:

l'agenda	agenda	le choléra	cholera	le pyjama	pyjamas
le bégonia	begonia	le cinéma	cinema	le visa	visa
le brouhaha	hubbub	l'opéra	opera		

However, there are a few exceptions:

la diva	diva	la saga	saga	la villa	villa
la polka	polka	la véranda	veranda		

Le choléra sévit dans cette région.	Cholera is rampant in this region.
Il faut un visa pour entrer dans ce pays.	You need a visa to enter this country.

This may be quite confusing, since we know that -a is generally a feminine ending in Romance languages. Indeed, French can be a bit peculiar, but there is an explanation. Unlike the other Romance languages, French did not keep the -a ending in Latin-derived feminine nouns.

-as

Nouns ending with -as are generally masculine:

le bras	arm	le fracas	crash, roar	le pas	step
le cadenas	padlock	le lilas	lilac	le repas	meal
le cas	case	le matelas	mattress	le verglas	glazed frost
l'embarras	embarrassment				

J'ai besoin d'un cadenas pour ma valise.	I need a padlock for my suitcase.
Alice a fait ses premiers pas à huit mois.	Alice made her first steps at the age of eight months.

-ème, -me, -ome, -ôme, -aume, -rme, -sme

Nouns ending in **-ème**, **-me**, **-ome**, **-ôme**, **-aume**, **-rme**, and **-sme** tend to be masculine:

le dôme	*dome*	**le problème**	*problem*	**le spasme**	*spasm*
l'idiome	*idiom*	**le royaume**	*kingdom*	**le terme**	*term*
le poème	*poem*				

Mon royaume pour un cheval!	*My kingdom for a horse!*
C'est **le** plus beau **poème** qu'il m'ait jamais écrit.	*It is the most beautiful poem he ever wrote to me.*

-ble, -cle, -gle, -ple

Nouns ending in **-ble**, **-cle**, **-gle**, and **-ple** are often masculine:

l'angle	*angle*	**le sable**	*sand*
le câble	*cable*	**le spectacle**	*show*
le périple	*journey*	**le temple**	*temple*

Here are some interesting exceptions, all with a Latin pedigree, except for **la bible**, a Greek interloper. The Greek neuter plural (*ta biblia*), which means *the books*, having become feminine in Romance languages because of its deceptive -**a** ending, was bound to become -**e** in French. Back to our Latin-derived exceptions:

French	English	Latin
la boucle	*buckle*	*buccula* (meaning *little mouth*)
la fable	*fable*	*fabula*
la règle	*rule*	*regula*
la table	*table*	*tabula*

Le spectacle ne dura qu'une heure.	*The show lasted only an hour.*
La boucle est bouclée.	*We have come full circle.*

-ac, -ak, -ic, -oc, -uc

Nouns ending in **-ac**, **-ak**, **-ic**, **-oc**, and **-uc** tend to be masculine:

l'ammoniac	*ammonia*	**le croc**	*fang/hook*	**le public**	*public*
l'aqueduc	*aqueduct*	**le diagnostic**	*diagnosis*	**le stuc**	*stucco*
l'armagnac	*Armagnac*	**le duc**	*duke*	**le tabac**	*tobacco*
le basilic	*basil*	**le fric**	*money/cash*	**le trafic**	*traffic*
le bivouac	*bivouac*	**le hamac**	*hammock*	**le troc**	*barter*
le bloc	*block, writing pad*	**le kayak**	*kayak*	**le truc**	*trick/thing/gimmick*
le clic	*click*	**le lac**	*lake*	**le viaduc**	*viaduct*

Renaud vient de penser à **un truc**.			*Renaud just thought of **something**.*
Tu as **un bloc** de papier?			*Do you have a writing **pad**?*

-g

Nouns ending in **-g** are generally masculine:

l'étang	*pond/lake*	**le joug**	*yoke*	**le sang**	*blood*
le faubourg	*suburb/ neighborhood*	**le rang**	*row/rank*		

Tristan a **du sang** sur sa chemise.	*Tristan has **blood** on his shirt.*
Célie est assise **au** troisième **rang**.	*Célie is sitting in **the** third **row**.*

-o, -op, -ort, -os, -ot, -ours, -us

Nouns ending in **-o**, **-op**, **-ort**, **-os**, **-ot**, **-ours**, and **-us** are usually masculine:

l'abricot	*apricot*	**l'escargot**	*snail*	**le numéro**	*number*
le cactus	*cactus*	**le jus**	*juice*	**l'ours**	*bear*
le coquelicot	*poppy*	**le lapsus**	*slip of the tongue*	**le paquebot**	*ocean liner*
le cours	*course*	**le lavabo**	*bathroom sink*	**le sirop**	*syrup*
le dos	*back*	**le mot**	*word*	**le sport**	*sport*
l'effort	*effort*	**le nimbus**	*nimbus cloud*	**le vélo**	*bicycle*

Quel numéro dois-je composer pour appeler Londres?	***What number** should I dial to call London?*
Vous devriez faire **un effort**!	*You should make **an effort**!*

Remember that gender does not change when a word is abbreviated:

la météo	*weather forecast*	**la photo**	*photography*	**la stéréo**	*hi-fi/stereo system*
la philo	*philosophy*	**la psycho**	*psychology*	**la vidéo**	*video*

La photo que tu as prise est un peu floue.	*The picture you took is a bit blurred.*
Comment il est, ton prof de **philo**?	*Your **philosophy** teacher, how is he?*

-ogue

Nouns ending in **-ogue** that refer to certain professionals may be masculine or feminine. For example, while Claude Lévi-Strauss was **un anthropologue** (*anthropologist*), we would call Margaret Mead **une anthropologue**.

Masculine nouns ending in -ogue

le catalogue	*catalog*	**l'épilogue**	*epilogue*
le dialogue	*dialogue*	**le prologue**	*prologue*

A hint: all these words are in some way derived from the Greek *logos*, a masculine noun that means *word,* and from many other words.

Feminine nouns ending in -ogue

la drogue	*drug*	**la synagogue**	*synagogue*
la morgue	*haughtiness/morgue*	**la vogue**	*fashion/vogue*
la pirogue	*pirogue, dug-out canoe*		

C'est **la** grande **vogue** maintenant.	*It's all **the rage** now.*
Les Gauthier ont descendu l'Amazone **en pirogue**.	*The Gauthiers went down the Amazon in **a pirogue**.*

-r, -er

Nouns ending in **-r** and **-er** are generally masculine:

l'avenir	*future*	**le cauchemar**	*nightmare*	**le jour**	*day*
le bar	*bar*	**le cuir**	*leather*	**le nénuphar**	*water lily*
le car	*bus/coach*	**le décor**	*décor*	**le tour**	*tour/trip/ride*
le castor	*beaver*	**le dollar**	*dollar*	**le trésor**	*treasure*

One exception to this rule is words ending in **-eur** when they do not denote a profession or a machine. Here are three additional exceptions:

la cour	*courtyard*
la star	*star, celebrity*
la tour	*tower*

C'était **le** pire **cauchemar** qu'on ait pu imaginer.	*It was **the** worst **nightmare** we could have imagined.*
Un sans-abri a découvert **un trésor** dans une grotte.	*A homeless man discovered **a treasure** in a grotto.*

-re

Nouns ending in **-re** are generally masculine:

le centre	*center*	**le lustre**	*luster/gloss*	**le mètre**	*meter*
le feutre	*felt*	**le maître**	*master/artist*	**le ventre**	*stomach, belly*
le filtre	*filter*				

These are some exceptions:

la fenêtre	*window*	**la lettre**	*letter*	**la vitre**	*window pane*
l'huître	*oyster*	**la montre**	*watch*		

Le centre culturel est juste à côté.	The cultural center is right next door.
Ne partez pas le ventre creux!	Don't leave with an empty stomach!

-x, -xe

For the most part, nouns ending in -x and -xe are masculine:

l'axe	*axis*	le flux	*flow, tide*	le luxe	*luxury*
le circonflexe	*circumflex*	l'inox	*stainless steel*	le lynx	*lynx*
le complexe	*complex*	le juke-box	*jukebox*	le paradoxe	*paradox*
l'équinoxe	*equinox*	le larynx	*larynx*	le sexe	*sex*

Here are some exceptions:

la boxe	*boxing*
la syntaxe	*syntax*
la taxe	*tax*

Interestingly, the word *syntax* is a derivation of the feminine Greek noun *taxis*, meaning *battle array*.

Tu oublies toujours le circonflexe sur « gâteau »!	You always forget the circumflex on gâteau!
Il vit dans le luxe.	He lives in luxury.

-e

Many nouns ending in -e are masculine, although there are some rather prominent feminine nouns in that category, such as **la gloire**. It is a mistake, however, to assume that the -e ending automatically defines a noun as feminine. Here are some examples:

l'ange	*angel*	le groupe	*group*	le pouce	*thumb*
le beurre	*butter*	le palace	*palace*	le souffle	*breath/blow*
le divorce	*divorce*	le peigne	*comb*	le verbe	*verb*
l'espace	*space*	le poste	*position/job*	le verre	*glass*

Tu préfères le beurre salé ou le beurre doux?	Do you prefer salted or unsalted butter?
Ce groupe est n'est pas compétent pour résoudre ce problème.	This group is not competent to solve this problem.

Here we are, at the end of the masculine endings. Ouf!

To facilitate the memorization of gender, make up sentences or rhymes like this one:

> Le soir, Lucas lis le journal dans son fauteuil et écoute le récital tandis que son chat joue avec le bouchon de la bouteille de son vin préféré.

> *At night, Lucas reads the paper in his armchair and listens to the recital while his cat plays with the cork from a bottle of his favorite wine.*

Repeat this sentence a few times, and you'll have a few endings engraved in your mind. Then create new ones or extract some from French literature. Write them in a small notebook or make a "Gender" list on your computer. You'll see—it works!

Basic feminine noun endings

The following nouns tend to be feminine:

-ade

l'ambassade	*embassy*	la limonade	*lemonade*
la cascade	*waterfall, stunt, series*	la promenade	*walk, ride*
la grenade	*grenade/pomegranate*	la salade	*salad*

Here are a few exceptions:

le grade	*rank, degree*
le jade	*jade*
le stade	*stadium*

L'ambassade n'est pas ouverte aujourd'hui.	*The Embassy is not open today.*
Moi, je prends la salade niçoise.	*I'm having the salad niçoise!*

-aie

la baie	*berry/bay/opening*	la monnaie	*change/currency*
la craie	*chalk*	la palmeraie	*palm grove*
la haie	*hedge/hurdle*	la taie	*pillowcase*

Leur jardin est entouré d'une haie d'aubépine.	*Their garden is surrounded with a hawthorn hedge.*
Auriez-vous de la monnaie?	*Could you give me some change?*

-aine

la douzaine	*dozen*	**la marraine**	*godmother*
la haine	*hatred*	**la migraine**	*migraine*
la laine	*wool*	**la semaine**	*week*

Here are a couple of exceptions:

le domaine	*estate, field/domain*
le Maine	*Maine*

Mathilde a acheté un tapis **de** haute **laine** à Marrakech.	*Mathilde bought a thick-pile **wool** rug in Marrakech.*
Offre-lui **une douzaine de** roses!	*Give her **a dozen** roses!*

-aison, -oison

la cloison	*partition, bulkhead, septum*	**la raison**	*reason, mind*
la conjugaison	*conjugation, union*	**la saison**	*season*
la maison	*house*	**la toison**	*fleece, mane*

Here are a few exceptions:

le poison	*poison*
le vison	*mink*

Connais-tu **la conjugaison** du verbe « s'asseoir »?	*Do you know **the conjugation** of the verb "to sit"?*
Jonathan se met en colère pour **une raison** ou une autre.	*Jonathan gets angry for **some reason** or other.*

-ence, -ance

la chance	*luck, chance*	**la puissance**	*power, authority*
l'indépendance	*independence*	**l'urgence**	*urgency, emergency*
la présidence	*presidency*	**la violence**	*violence, roughness*

Here is an exception: **le silence** (*silence*).

Vous avez de **la chance** d'aller en France demain.	*You are **lucky** to go to France tomorrow.*
Ils ont lutté pour **leur indépendance**.	*They fought for **their independence**.*

-ande

l'amande	almond, kernel	la demande	request, application
la bande	band/bandage//group	la viande	meat
la commande	order, control		

Julien a envoyé **sa demande** hier.
Ma commande n'est pas encore arrivée.

*Julien sent **his application** yesterday.*
***My order** has not arrived yet.*

-ée

l'année	year	la durée	duration
l'araignée	spider	l'idée	idea
la bouée	rubber ring, buoy	la journée	day

Here are a few exceptions:

l'apogée	apogee/peak	le mausolée	mausoleum
l'athée	atheist	le musée	museum
le colisée	coliseum	le rez-de-chaussée	main floor
le lycée	high school	le trophée	trophy

Quelles idées folles!
Quelle sera **la durée** du vol?

***What* crazy *ideas*!**
*What's **the duration** of the flight?*

Words indicating quantity are often feminine:

une assiettée	plateful	une cuillerée	spoonful
une bouchée	mouthful	une pelletée	shovelful
une brassée	armful	une pincée	pinch
une brouettée	wheelbarrowful	une poignée	handful

Sofia est arrivée avec **une brassée** de fleurs
    sauvages.
Maheu m'a donné **une poignée** de cerises.

*Sofia arrived with **an armful** of wild*
    flowers.
*Maheu gave me **a handful** of cherries.*

-esse, -osse, -ousse

la brosse	brush	la politesse	politeness
la housse	cover	la sagesse	wisdom
la jeunesse	youth	la trousse	case

Here are a couple of exceptions:

le carrosse	coach
le pamplemousse	grapefruit

Florin, c'est la voix de **la sagesse**.

Florin, he is the voice of **wisdom**.

J'ai perdu un bouton. Tu as **une trousse à** couture?

I lost a button. Do you have **a sewing kit**?

-ette

l'assiette	*plate, basis*	**la fourchette**	*fork/margin*
la dette	*debt*	**la noisette**	*hazelnut, small knob*
la devinette	*riddle*	**la serviette**	*towel/napkin*

Here are some interesting exceptions:

le bébé-éprouvette	*test-tube baby*	**le quartette**	*quartet*
le casse-noisette	*nutcracker*	**le quintette**	*quintet*
le porte-serviette	*napkin holder*	**le squelette**	*skeleton*

Diego a **une dette** de reconnaissance envers vous.

Diego has **a debt** of gratitude toward you.

Donne-moi **une** plus grande **asssiette**.

Give me **a larger plate**.

-eur (excluding nouns denoting professions and machines)

la chaleur	*heat*	**la lueur**	*glow, light*
la couleur	*color, light*	**la peur**	*fear*
la fleur	*flower*	**la tumeur**	*tumor*

Here are some exceptions:

le bonheur	*happiness*	**le labeur**	*labor/toil*
l'honneur	*honor*	**le malheur**	*misfortune/ordeal*

Margaux a **une peur** bleue des souris.

Margaux is **scared** to death of mice.

De **quelle couleur** allez-vous repeindre votre salle de bain?

What color are you going to repaint your bathroom?

-ie, -rie

la magie	*magic*	**la thérapie**	*therapy*
la poésie	*poetry, poem*	**l'utopie**	*utopia*
la tapisserie	*tapestry, wallpaper*	**la vie**	*life*

More exceptions to add to the list include:

le génie	*genius*	**le parapluie**	*umbrella*
l'incendie	*fire*	**le sosie**	*double*
le messie	*messiah*	**le zombie**	*zombie*

Marie Laveau croit à **la magie**.   *Marie Laveau believes in **magic**.*
La thérapie de Lola a duré cinq ans.   *Lola's **therapy** lasted five years.*

-ise

la cerise	cherry	la gourmandise	delicacy, greediness
la chemise	shirt, folder	la surprise	surprise
la crise	crisis, attack, fit	la valise	suitcase, bag

La crise financière a eu un impact catastrophique sur cette province.
*The financial **crisis** had a terrible impact on this province.*

Je pense que **ta valise** est trop lourde.
*I think **your suitcase** is too heavy.*

-aille

la bataille	battle, fight	la médaille	medal, disk
l'écaille	scale, chip, flake	la paille	straw
la faille	flaw/fault (geology)	la taille	waist/size/height

An exception is **le braille** (*Braille*). This exception could be explained by the fact that the Braille alphabet was named after its inventor, Louis Braille (1809–1852).

C'est trop serré à **la taille**.   *It is too tight around **the waist**.*
Il y a **une faille** dans votre argument.   *There is **a flaw** in your argument.*

-ille

la brindille	twig	la lentille	lens/lentil
la famille	family	la myrtille	bilberry
la fille	girl, daughter	la vanille	vanilla

Here is a trio of exceptions:

le gorille	gorilla/bodyguard
le quadrille	quadrille
le vaudeville	vaudeville

Manon ne veut pas de **lentilles** mais une glace à **la vanille**.
*Manon does not want **lentils** but a **vanilla** ice cream cone.*

La famille d'Hadrien habite à Nîmes.
*Hadrien's **family** lives in Nîmes.*

-ouille

la brouille	disagreement	la nouille	noodles
la citrouille	pumpkin	la patrouille	patrol
la grenouille	frog	la ratatouille	ratatouille

La ratatouille de votre grand-mère est délicieuse.		*Your grandmother's **ratatouille** is delicious.*	
La grenouille est assise sur **une citrouille** près du lac.		*The frog is sitting on **a pumpkin** near the lake.*	

-ique

la botanique	*botany*	**la polémique**	*controversy*
la musique	*music*	**la politique**	*politics, policy*
la physique	*physics*	**la république**	*republic*

Here are quite a few exceptions:

l'antibiotique	*antibiotic*	**le plastique**	*plastic*
le lexique	*glossary*	**le portique**	*portico*
le moustique	*mosquito*	**le téléphérique**	*cable-car*
le pique-nique	*picnic*		

Quelle musique écoutez-vous?	*What music do you listen to?*
Cette politique est fort dangereuse.	*This policy is quite dangerous.*

Many **-ique** words come from Latin feminine nouns ending in *-ica*, such as *musica* and *res publica*. However, as we have seen, **-ique** words come to us from other languages as well, so one needs to tread gingerly.

-gion, -nion, -sion, -ssion

la compréhension	*understanding*	**l'opinion**	*opinion*
la décision	*decision*	**la passion**	*passion*
l'occasion	*chance/opportunity*	**la région**	*region*

Damien n'a **aucune compréhension** de la situation.	*Damien has **no understanding** of the situation.*
Antonin doit se faire **une opinion** sur la situation.	*Antonin must form **an opinion** on the situation.*

-tion, -xion

la connexion	*connection*	**la population**	*population*
la génération	*generation*	**la révolution**	*revolution*
l'information	*information, piece of news*	**la tradition**	*tradition, legend*

Here are a few exceptions:

l'avion	*airplane*
le champion	*champion*
le bastion	*bastion/stronghold*

Ils sont fidèles à **la tradition**.	*They are true to **tradition**.*
La Révolution française a eu lieu en 1789.	*The French **Revolution** took place in 1789.*

Why doesn't **avion**, you may ask, share the feminine gender of the other Latin-based words on this list, such as **population** or **tradition**? Well, **avion** is different because it is a neologism, an artificial construction, just like **logiciel**.

When the airplane was invented, people scrambled to find the right word. English speakers could not come up with anything better than the vaguely Latinate *aeroplane*, or *airplane*, which was less cumbersome than the German *das Flugzeug* but still far from perfect. Fortunately, French speakers know how to benefit from their visceral connection to Latin, which non-Romance languages can only dream about. In fact, **avion**, a construction based on the feminine Latin noun *avis*, which means *bird*, exemplifies the facility with which French incorporates the stupendously rich Latin vocabulary into its own lexicon. This proves the thesis, advanced by the great German literary scholar Ernst Robert Curtius, that Latin words in the French vocabulary are not loan words, since the source language is not foreign.

-ite

l'appendicite	*appendicitis*	**la limite**	*border, limit, edge*
la conduite	*behavior/conduct*	**la marguerite**	*daisy*
l'élite	*elite*	**la réussite**	*success*

Here is a list of exceptions:

l'anthracite	*anthracite*	**le satellite**	*satellite*
le gîte	*shelter/home*	**le site**	*area, site*
l'insolite	*unusual*	**le sulfite**	*sulphite*
le mérite	*merit*	**le termite**	*termite*
le rite	*rite*		

Au-delà de **cette limite**, votre billet n'est plus valable.	*Beyond **this limit**, your ticket is no longer valid.*
C'est un signe de **réussite sociale**.	*It's a sign of **social success**.*

-té, -tié

l'amitié	friendship	la pitié	pity, mercy
la cécité	blindness	la santé	health
la laïcité	secularism	la virilité	virility

Here are more exceptions to learn:

l'aparté	private conversation/aside	l'été	summer
l'arrêté	decree	le karaté	karate
le côté	side		

As mentioned earlier, some feminine nouns with these endings stem from Latin nouns ending in -a, such as *amicitia*.

La laïcité est un sujet controversé en France.	*Secularism is a controversial topic in France.*
Leur **amitié** fut éternelle.	*Their friendship was eternal.*

Here's a helpful hint: most feminine **-té** words have English cognates ending in -ty, a suffix that was stolen from French.

l'identité	identity	la nationalité	nationality
l'illégalité	illegality	la propriété	property
la liberté	freedom/liberty	la vanité	vanity

Quelle est **la nationalité** de Morgan?	*What's Morgan's nationality?*
Ulysse a agi en **toute liberté**.	*Ulysse acted with complete freedom.*

Here are three exceptions:

le comité	committee
le comté	county
le traité	treaty

Le traité aurait été signé pendant la nuit.	*The treaty was reportedly signed during the night.*
Le comité de soutien se réunira ce soir.	*The support committee will meet tonight.*

-ode

la commode	chest of drawers	l'ode	ode
la méthode	method	la pagode	pagoda
la mode	fashion/style	la période	period/time

Here some exceptions:

l'antipode	antipode	l'exode	exodus
le code	code	le mode	mode, mood, method
l'épisode	episode/serial/phase		

Quelle est **la** meilleure **méthode** pour mémoriser le genre des noms?	*What's **the** best **method** to memorize the gender of nouns?*
Plusieurs femmes priaient dans **la pagode**.	*Several women were praying in **the pagoda**.*

-tude

l'attitude	attitude	l'inquiétude	anxiety, worry
l'étude	study	la longitude	longitude
l'habitude	habit	la solitude	solitude/loneliness

Here are a couple of exceptions:

le prélude	prelude
l'interlude	interlude

Many French nouns with these endings come from feminine Latin words ending in *-tudo*, such as *solitudo*. The exceptions can be explained by the fact that these words are compounds containing the Latin word *ludus* (*game*), which is masculine.

Blaise, tu devrais te débarrasser de **cette** mauvaise **habitude**.	*Blaise, you should get rid of **this** bad **habit**.*
Ophélie aime **la solitude**.	*Ophélie loves being **by herself**.*

-ure

la censure	censorship, censure	la nature	nature
l'écriture	writing	la peinture	paint/painting
la lecture	reading	la voiture	car

You'll need to remember these exceptions:

l'augure	omen	le murmure	whisper/murmur
le cyanure	cyanide	le parjure	traitor

Cédric vient de vendre **une** autre **peinture** à l'huile.	*Cédric just sold **another** oil **painting**.*
La meilleure recette pour apprendre le français, c'est **la lecture** et **l'écriture**.	*The best recipe for learning French is **reading** and **writing**.*

Note: Just like -**tié**, which we have seen in **amitié**, the French ending -**re**, like in **nature**, stems from the Latin ending -*ra*, found in such eminently feminine words as *natura*. One of our exceptions, **l'augure**, also comes from Latin, but the original word is *augurium*, which is neuter. The only thing about the neuter we need to know is that Latin words in this gender automatically become masculine in French.

Incidentally, according to the Belgian philologist André Goosse, editor of the famed *Bon usage*, the fact that the masculine in French is a default gender for the Latin neuter undermines the notion that the masculine gender in French implies power. For example, the neuter *medicamentum* becomes **médicament**, a masculine noun in French. Whenever you think of English words ending in -*um*, more specifically the Latin words that seem to enjoy a green card status in English, words such as *colloquium* and *opprobrium*, you can be sure that their French equivalents, in this case **le colloque** and **l'opprobre**, are masculine.

Other cases

There are many other endings, and each must be studied case by case.

-ice

Nouns ending in -**ice**, except for the feminine forms of masculine words to denote people practicing particular professions, such as **rédactrice** (*female editor*) or **directrice** (*female director*), are often masculine:

le bénéfice	*benefit*	**l'exercice**	*exercise*	**le service**	*service*
le caprice	*caprice*	**l'indice**	*clue*	**le solstice**	*solstice*
le complice	*accomplice*	**le précipice**	*precipice*	**le vice**	*vice*
le dentifrice	*toothpaste*				

But watch out for the feminine nouns:

l'avarice	*greed*	**l'épice**	*spice*
la cicatrice	*scar*	**la malice**	*malice, mischievousness*

This looks like a rule that's not really a rule. However, we can get some help from an old friend, Latin. You see, as mentioned earlier, the French masculine nouns, in their old (i.e., Latin) form as neuter nouns ended in -*um*: *beneficium* (**le bénéfice**), *indicium* (**l'indice**), *servitium* (**le service**), *solstitium* (**le solstice**), and *vitium* (**le vice**).

Now what about those pesky feminine nouns? Well, as we know, French likes to standardize noun endings, which explains why feminine Latin nouns such as *avaritia* (**l'avarice**), *cicatrix* (**la cicatrice**), and *malitia* (**la malice**), also ended up with -**ice** endings. Sometimes one has the impression (French is no exception) that languages have a mind of their own, often ignoring our wishes and desires. Frustrating, you may say, but a certain measure of unpredictability also makes languages fascinating and exciting.

La police a arrêté **le complice** du meurtrier.	*The police arrested **the murderer's accomplice**.*
Pourriez-vous me rendre **un service**?	*Could you do me **a favor**?*

-aire, -oire

We could try to make a rule for **-aire** and **-oire** being masculine:

l'anniversaire	*birthday*	l'interrogatoire	*questioning/cross-examination*
le dictionnaire	*dictionary*		
le formulaire	*form*	le laboratoire	*laboratory*
		le mémoire	*thesis/dissertation*

However, we cannot avoid the many androgynous words, such as **le/la stagiaire** (*intern*) and a very long list of exceptions. Here are a few of them:

l'affaire	*business, issue*	la foire	*fair*	la moustiquaire	*mosquito screen*
la baignoire	*bathtub*	la grammaire	*grammar*	la victoire	*victory*
la bouilloire	*kettle*	la mémoire	*memory*		

You might be better off making your own rhymes.

Le stagiaire, fatigué d'écrire **son mémoire** le jour de **son anniversaire**, a pris un bain dans **sa baignoire** avant d'aller à **la foire** artisanale.	*Tired of working on **his thesis** on **his birthday**, the intern took a bath in **his tub** and went to the arts and crafts **fair**.*
Quel interrogatoire! Ça a duré plus d'une semaine!	***What a cross-examination!** It lasted more than a week!*
Remplissez d'abord **le formulaire**!	*Fill in **the form** first!*

-oi, -ois, -oix

The only feminine nouns ending in **-oi**, **-ois**, and **-oix** are:

la croix	*cross*	la loi	*law*	la paroi	*wall/partition*
la foi	*faith*	la noix	*nut*	la voix	*voice*

Elles parlaient à **voix basse**.	*They were talking in **low voices**.*
C'est **la loi** de la jungle.	*It's **the law** of the jungle.*

-f, -aim

The only feminine nouns ending in **-f** and **-aim** are:

la clef ou **la clé**	*key*	**la nef**	*nave*
la faim	*hunger*	**la soif**	*thirst*

La faim dans le monde empire chaque jour.	*World **hunger** gets worse every day.*
Où as-tu mis **la clé** du coffre-fort?	*Where did you put **the key** of the safe?*

-ole, -ôle, -ule

Nouns ending in **-ole**, **-ôle**, or **-ule** seem willing to go either way. While Latin may provide some guidance, there is no foolproof method. Nevertheless, it helps to know that *symbolus*—**le symbole** (*symbol*)—is masculine in Latin and *crepusculum*—**le crépuscule** (*dusk*)—is neuter, while *schola*—**l'école** (*school*)—is feminine.

Masculine nouns ending in -**ole** or -**ôle**:

le contrôle	*control*	**le pactole**	*fortune/gold mine*	**le protocole**	*protocol*
le monopole	*monopoly*	**le pôle**	*pole*	**le symbole**	*symbol*

Feminine nouns ending in -**ole** or -**ôle**:

l'Acropole	*Acropolis*	**la console**	*console*	**l'idole**	*idol*
la banderole	*banner*	**l'école**	*school*	**la nécropole**	*necropolis*
la casserole	*pan*	**la gondole**	*gondola*	**la parole**	*speech*

Masculine nouns ending in -**ule**:

le crépuscule	*dusk*	**le préambule**	*preamble*	**le scrupule**	*scruple*
l'émule	*emulator*	**le ridicule**	*absurdity/*	**le véhicule**	*vehicle*
le funambule	*tightrope walker*		*ridiculousness*	**le vestibule**	*hall/lobby*

Feminine nouns ending in -**ule**:

la canicule	*heat wave*	**la majuscule**	*upper case/capital*	**la pilule**	*pill*
la cellule	*cell*	**la mule**	*mule*	**la spatule**	*spatula*
la formule	*formula*	**la pellicule**	*film/dandruff*	**la tentacule**	*tentacle*
la libellule	*dragonfly*	**la péninsule**	*peninsula*		

Ils ont fait le tour de Venise dans **une gondole** bleu nuit.	*They toured Venice in **a midnight blue gondola.***
Une libellule voletait au-dessus d'un champ de maïs.	***A dragonfly** was fluttering over a cornfield.*

-iste, -que

Nouns ending in **-iste** and **-que** that refer to persons can be either masculine or feminine:

le/la paysagiste	*landscape artist*	**le/la scientifique**	*scientist*	**le/la violoniste**	*violinist*
le/la scénariste	*scriptwriter*	**le/la spécialiste**	*specialist*		

Other nouns ending in **-iste** are feminine:

la liste	*list*
la piste	*track/path*

Agnès Varda est l'une **des** plus grandes **scénaristes** du cinéma français.	*Agnès Varda is one of **the** greatest **scriptwriters** of French cinema.*
Fais **une liste** de tout ce dont on a besoin d'acheter.	*Make **a list** of everything we need to buy.*

Nouns derived from past participles

Nouns derived from adjectives and the masculine forms of the past participle are masculine:

l'aîné	*the oldest*	**le favori**	*the favorite*	**le nu**	*naked*
le beau	*the handsome one*	**l'inconnu**	*the unknown*	**le vécu**	*lived experience*
le bien	*good*	**le mal**	*evil*	**le vieux**	*the old one*
le détenu	*prisoner*				

Nouns derived from adjectives and the feminine forms of past participles are feminine:

la belle	*the beautiful*	**la mariée**	*the bride*	**la venue**	*the coming*
la crue	*flood*	**la petite**	*the little one*	**la vue**	*vision*
la disparue	*the vanished one*	**la retraitée**	*the retiree*		

Ce que le lecteur veut, c'est **du vécu**.	*What the reader wants is **real-life experience**.*
La mariée était si belle dans sa robe d'organdi.	***The bride** was so beautiful in her organdy dress.*

EXERCICE

1·1

Indiquer le genre en ajoutant l'article défini.

1. _____ tolérance

2. _____ pain

3. _____ compliment

4. _____ sapin

5. _____ présence

6. _____ courage

7. _____ agneau

8. _____ orangeraie

9. _____ chaîne

10. _____ plage

11. _____ ruisseau

12. _____ architecture

13. _____ classement

14. _____ symbolisme

15. _____ égalité

16. _____ odeur

17. _____ pudeur

18. _____ vignoble

19. _____ paille

20. _____ calepin

EXERCICE

1·2

Compléter cette comptine avec l'article défini, masculin ou féminin, et traduire les adjectifs possessifs.

J'aime _____ eau

J'aime _____ eau dans _____ (my) baignoire

Et sur _____ carrelage de _____ cuisine quand maman le nettoie

J'aime _____ eau sur _____ plage

J'aime les vaguelettes

Qui me chatouillent les doigts de pied

Et s'en vont avec _____ marée

J'aime _____ eau des flaques et des étangs

Des lacs et des barrages où elle se heurte en écumant

J'aime _____ pluie qui me mouille _____ langue

Et qui fait pousser les plantes dans _____ jardin

J'aime _____ eau des fleuves

_____ eau où pullulent les petits poissons

J'aime _____ eau quand elle est bien chaude

_____ matin dans _____ (my) lavabo

J'aime _____ eau quand elle est gelée

Quand je peux patiner sur les mares glacées.

EXERCICE
1·3

Indiquer le genre de ces noms en ajoutant l'article défini.

1. _____ meuble

2. _____ soja

3. _____ référence

4. _____ cocktail

5. _____ rail

6. _____ fin

7. _____ attitude

8. _____ lainage

9. _____ parlement

10. _____ centaine

11. _____ sculpture

12. _____ libéralisme

13. _____ signal

14. _____ délicatesse

15. _____ horlogerie

16. _____ citadin

17. _____ tact

18. _____ orthographe

19. _____ clavecin

20. _____ fraternité

Indiquer le genre de ces noms en ajoutant l'article défini.

1. _____ acacia

2. _____ chanson

3. _____ portefeuille

4. _____ domino

5. _____ signature

6. _____ écaille

7. _____ millefeuille

8. _____ cinéma

9. _____ tribu

10. _____ tracteur

11. _____ établissement

12. _____ altitude

13. _____ hamac

14. _____ ghetto

15. _____ confirmation

16. _____ noix

17. _____ main

18. _____ inclinaison

19. _____ soif

20. _____ faim

What are you doing?

Naming people and animals

As a rule, professions are masculine when they refer to a man and feminine when they refer to a woman. You can just add a final **e**:

l'apprenti/	*apprentice*	**l'avocat/**	*lawyer*
l'apprentie		**l'avocate**	
l'attaché/	*attaché*	**le magistrat/**	*magistrate,*
l'attachée		**la magistrate**	*judge*

In the past, traditionally masculine professions, even if practiced by women, remained masculine:

le compositeur	*composer*	**le procureur**	*prosecutor*
le peintre	*painter*	**le professeur**	*professor/*
			teacher

In 1998, Lionel Jospin, the socialist prime minister, created a new commission to study the question. *Femme, j'écris ton nom,* the commission's resulting guide for the feminization of professions and titles, was published in 1999. If you are an insomniac, you may enjoy reading this hundred-page guide of some obscure professions in French or in English, which is available online. The guide had a major impact.

In addition, Quebec, at the cutting edge of feminization, played a key role, even if we, the French, won't admit it. . . . Over ten years ago, I started consulting and hosting workshops for the Blue Metropolis Montreal International Festival. I gasped when I saw myself listed in the festival's program as «**Annie Heminway, *professeure* à New York.**» I have to admit it took me some time to get used to it.

These days, you will read more frequently in the newspapers and magazines: **l'écrivaine** (*writer*), **l'ingénieure** (*engineer*), **la juge** (*judge*). Even the newspaper *Le Monde* talks about a famous writer as **l'écrivaine** Léonora Miano.

You have to use caution, though. Were you to send a letter to a minister of the government, you should ask the Chief of Protocol if she uses **Madame le ministre** or **Madame la ministre**. In a speech made by Roselyne Bachelot on January 2008, for example, the headline was: « **Discours** de *Madame le ministre* de la santé, de la jeunesse et des sports. » Then Roselyne Bachelot herself had written, a few lines down: « *La ministre* de la qualité des soins que je veux être ne peut que reprendre à son compte de tels propos. » As you can see, anything goes! The tendency today, however, is to use **Madame la ministre**.

Human beings

One way of identifying the nouns is to learn if they have identical or different root words.

Identical roots

In numerous cases, the noun of a profession is identical in the masculine and the feminine:

l'architecte/l'architecte	*architect*
le vétérinaire/la vétérinaire	*veterinarian*
le dentiste/la dentiste	*dentist*

In many instances, you add an **-e** at the end of the noun:

l'avocat/l'avocate	*lawyer*
le marchand/la marchande	*merchant*
l'associé/l'associée	*partner*

In other cases, there are many possible endings depending on the noun. Here are some examples, but always check in the dictionary.

l'ouvrier/l'ouvrière	*worker*
le conseiller/la conseillère	*adviser*
le chocolatier/la chocolatière	*chocolate maker*
l'acheteur/l'acheteuse	*buyer*
le vendeur/la vendeuse	*salesperson*
le coiffeur/la coiffeuse	*hairdresser*
le musicien/la musicienne	*musician*
le doyen/la doyenne	*dean, most senior member*
le pharmacien/la pharmacienne	*pharmacist*
le rédacteur/la rédactrice	*editor*
le concepteur/la conceptrice	*designer, project manager*
le spectateur/la spectatrice	*viewer, member of an audience*

le patron/la patronne	*boss*
le baron/la baronne	*baron*
le vigneron/la vigneronne	*wine grower*
le prince/la princesse	*prince/princess*
le maître/la maîtresse	*master/mistress*
le comte/la comtesse	*count/countess*

If there is an adjective, it will agree accordingly:

le directeur financier/la directrice financière	*financial director*

La coiffeuse d'Alice est aussi **musicienne**.	*Alice's **hairdresser** is also a **musician**.*
Les ouvriers ont demandé une augmentation à **leur patronne**.	*The workers asked **their boss** for a raise.*

EXERCICE

2·1

Elle fait le même métier que son cousin, donc elle est...

1. Il est directeur. Elle est _____.

2. Il est chanteur. Elle est _____.

3. Il est gardien. Elle est _____.

4. Il est commerçant. Elle est _____.

5. Il est pédiatre. Elle est _____.

6. Il est consultant. Elle est _____.

7. Il est traducteur. Elle est _____.

8. Il est agriculteur. Elle est _____.

9. Il est technicien. Elle est _____.

10. Il est psychologue. Elle est _____.

11. Il est assistant technique. Elle est _____.

12. Il est astrologue. Elle est _____.

13. Il est mécanicien. Elle est _____.

14. Il est boucher. Elle est _____.

15. Il est électricien. Elle est _____.

16. Il est archiduc. Elle est _____.

17. Il est dessinateur. Elle est _____.

18. Il est baron. Elle est _____.

19. Il est infirmier. Elle est _____.

20. Il est viticulteur. Elle est _____.

Different root words

Sometimes the basis for the masculine and the feminine is different or the root word happens to be different.

le beau-frère/la belle-sœur	*brother-in-law/sister-in-law*
le beau-père/la belle-mère	*father-in-law, stepfather/mother-in-law, stepmother*
le garçon/la fille	*boy/girl*
le gendre/la belle-fille	*son-in-law/daughter-in-law*
l'homme/la femme	*man/woman*
le mari/la femme	*husband/wife*
l'oncle/la tante	*uncle/aunt*
le parrain/la marraine	*godfather/godmother*
le père/la mère	*father/mother*
le roi/la reine	*king/queen*

Le cardinal de Mazarin fut **le parrain** de Louis XIV.	*Cardinal Mazarin was Louis XIV's **godfather**.*
C'est triste mais Corrine ne s'entend pas avec **son gendre**.	*It is sad but Corrine does not get along with **her son-in-law**.*

Some nouns follow no rule:

le barman/	*barman/*	**la couturière**	*seamstress*
la barmaid	*barmaid*	**le steward/**	*flight attendant*
le couturier	*couturier/*	**l'hôtesse de l'air**	
	fashion designer		

Coco Chanel était **un** grand **couturier**.	*Coco Chanel was **a great fashion designer**.*

As mentioned in the introduction, the feminization of nouns is widespread. And yet, the masculine form is still used by a lot of women. You may want to ask for the business card of the woman you are talking to so you'll have an answer as to which she prefers.

Here are more professions that are often feminized. But always ask to double-check.

l'acuponcteur/ l'acuponctrice	acupuncturist	l'inventeur/ l'inventrice	inventor
le chirurgien/ la chirurgienne	surgeon	le poète/ la poétesse	poet
le compositeur/ la compositrice	composer	le sculpteur/ la sculpteure or la sculptrice	sculptor
l'écrivain/l'écrivaine	writer		

Catherine a obtenu son diplôme d'**acuponctrice** à Paris.

Agnès Vincent est une talentueuse **compositrice** de musique de film.

*Catherine got her **acupuncture** diploma in Paris.*

*Agnès Vincent is a talented film **composer**.*

Masculine nouns for both men and women

Some nouns are always masculine whether referring to a man or a woman:

l'acolyte	acolyte/associate	le chef	leader, boss	le mannequin	model
l'agresseur	attacker	le clerc	clerk	le monarque	monarch
l'ange	angel	le déserteur	deserter	le sauveur	savior
l'apôtre	apostle	le forçat	convict	le successeur	successor
l'assassin	murderer	le génie	genius	le témoin	witness
le bandit	bandit	le goinfre	glutton	le tyran	tyrant
le brigand	brigand	le gourmet	epicure	le vandale	vandal
le charlatan	charlatan, quack	l'imposteur	impostor	le voyou	hooligan, rascal

Violène est **un** beau **mannequin**.
La femme de Louis est **un ange**.

*Violène is **a beautiful model**.*
*Louis's **wife** is **an angel**.*

Feminine nouns for both men and women

Some nouns are always feminine whether referring to a man or a woman:

l'Altesse	Highness	l'étoile	star, leading dancer	la personne	person
l'autorité	authority	l'idole	idol	la star	star
la célébrité	celebrity	la Majesté	Majesty	la vedette	star

l'égérie	*muse*	**la personnalité**	*prominent figure*
l'éminence grise	*gray eminence*	**la victime**	*victim*

Gérard Depardieu est **une des** plus grandes **vedettes** du cinéma.

Gérard Depardieu is **one of the** greatest movie **stars**.

Bernard Kouchner a toujours été **l'égérie** de la gauche.

Bernard Kouchner has always been **an iconic figure** of the left.

Feminine nouns used only for men

Some feminine nouns are used only for men:

la brute	*bully, boor*	**la crapule**	*villain, crook*	**Son Éminence**	*His Eminence*
la canaille	*scoundrel*	**l'huile**	*big shot, bigwig*	**Sa Sainteté**	*His Holiness*

Ce type, c'est **une** véritable **crapule**.

This guy is **a** real **crook**.

Son Éminence Dzogchen Rinpoché a participé à une conférence avec le Dalai Lama à Toulouse.

His Eminence Dzogchen Rinpoché took part in a conference with the Dalai Lama in Toulouse.

In the army, some terms that were used only for men in the past are applicable for women today.

l'estafette	*courier*	**la recrue**	*recruit*	**la vigie**	*lookout/watch*
l'ordonnance	*orderly*	**la sentinelle**	*sentry/sentinel*		

EXERCICE
2·2

Compléter avec l'article indéfini *un* ou *une*.

1. Son cousin est _____ célébrité dans le monde du spectacle.

2. _____ altesse royale que nous n'avons pas vraiment reconnue, a fait halte dans notre village hier.

3. Ta tante est _____ ange!

4. Mathieu est _____ personne sur qui on peut compter.

5. Sandrine est _____ mannequin célèbre pour ses coiffures excentriques.

6. Monsieur Thibault est _____ génie en informatique.

7. Sa femme est _____ gourmet par excellence.

8. Ce chanteur, c'est _____ idole depuis des années.

9. Ce type, c'est _____ véritable crapule!

10. Julie est _____ témoin que le juge veut entendre.

EXERCICE
2·3

Mettre l'adjectif possessif *son* ou *sa* devant le nom.

1. L'impresario et _____ star prenaient un verre sur la Croisette.

2. Mélanie voudrait inviter _____ oncle et _____ tante pour son anniversaire.

3. La police n'a pas encore retrouvé _____ assassin.

4. Hervé est arrivé avec Anna, _____ successeur.

5. Alice, tu es _____ sauveur!

6. _____ parrain lui a offert un joli bracelet.

7. Lui et _____ acolyte, ils ne font que des bêtises!

8. Yan est venu nous voir avec _____ beau-frère et _____ belle-mère.

9. Ce pays ne peut pas se débarrasser de _____ tyran.

10. Quelle est _____ vedette préférée?

Some nouns used only for men

The following nouns are used only for men:

le bandit	*bandit*	**le confrère**	*colleague*	**le garçon**	*boy*
le baryton	*baritone*	**le curé**	*priest*	**le mousquetaire**	*musketeer*
le cardinal	*cardinal*	**le dictateur**	*dictator*	**le page**	*page*
le castrat	*castrato*	**l'éphèbe**	*beautiful young man, Adonis*	**le parrain**	*godfather*

le chapelain	chaplain	l'escroc	swindler	le père	father
le charlatan	charlatan	l'évêque	bishop	le ténor	tenor
le compère	accomplice, buddy	le fils	son	le valet	manservant

Le parrain de **notre** fille est Grégoire.	**Our** daughter's **godfather** is Grégoire.
Ce moine tibétain vit à Dharmsala, en Inde.	**This** Tibetan **monk** lives in Dharmsala, in India.

Some nouns used only for women

The following nouns are used only for women:

l'accouchée	new mother	la danseuse étoile	prima ballerina	la mère	mother
l'amazone	amazon, horsewoman	la diva	diva	la midinette	starry-eyed girl
la ballerine	ballet dancer	la femme	woman, wife	la muse	muse
la Bigoudène	Bigouden woman	la fille	girl, daughter	la naïade	naiad
la bonne	maid	la marâtre	cruel mother	la nourrice	wet nurse, nurse
la cantatrice	opera singer	la marraine	godmother		
la commère	gossip	la matrone	matron	la nounou	nanny
la consœur	female colleague	la mégère	shrew	la sage-femme	midwife

Comment s'appelle **la nounou** d'Alice?	*What's the name of Alice's **nanny**?*
Sylvie Guillem est **l'une des** meilleures **danseuses étoiles** françaises.	*Sylvie Guillem is **one of the** best French **prima ballerinas**.*

EXERCICE
2·4

Compléter avec l'article défini *le* ou *la*.

1. _____ nourrice de Félix est irlandaise.

2. Marc et _____ confrère de Vincent assisteront au colloque.

3. Au vernissage se trouvaient Picasso avec _____ muse d'Aragon.

4. C'est _____ escroc que j'ai vu dans le journal!

5. _____ cantatrice que vous rencontrerez ce soir interprètera Aïda à l'Opéra Bastille en mars.

6. Avez-vous vu _____ valet?

7. _____ vandale, tout vêtu de noir, a commencé à briser les vitres des voitures.

8. _____ moine à l'entrée du monastère sera notre guide.

9. Comment s'appelle _____ baryton qui chantera Madame Butterfly?

10. _____ Bigoudène vend des galettes au marché de Quimper.

Animals

Since the animal kingdom, just like the human world, has genders, one usually has to learn two nouns for each species.

Animal couples with identical root words

Couples may be made of the male noun plus different suffixes:

agneau/agnelle	*lamb/ewe lamb*	**hérisson/hérissonne**	*hedgehog*
âne/ânesse	*donkey/she-donkey*	**héron/héronne**	*heron*
buffle/bufflonne	*buffalo*	**lapin/lapine**	*rabbit/doe rabbit*
chameau/chamelle	*camel/she-camel*	**lion/lionne**	*lion/lioness*
chat/chatte	*cat/she-cat*	**loup/louve**	*wolf/she-wolf*
chevreuil/chevrette	*roebuck/roe deer*	**ours/ourse**	*bear/she-bear*
chien/chienne	*dog/female dog*	**renard/renarde**	*fox/vixen*
éléphant/éléphante	*elephant/cow elephant*	**paon/paonne**	*peacock/peahen*
faisan/faisane	*pheasant/hen pheasant*	**tigre/tigresse**	*tiger/tigress*

Les enfants ont vu **une ourse polaire** et **un chameau** au zoo.

The children saw **a polar she-bear** and **a camel** at the zoo.

François, **le chat** de Michael, aime s'asseoir sur le clavier de l'ordinateur.

*François, Michael's **cat**, likes to sit on the computer keyboard.*

Animal couples with different root words

Some male and female nouns of animals are totally different, just as in English:

bélier/brebis	*ram/ewe*	**dindon/dinde**	*turkey/turkey hen*
bouc/chèvre	*goat/she-goat*	**jars/oie**	*gander/goose*
canard/cane	*duck/female duck*	**porc/truie**	*hog/sow*

cerf/biche	*stag/doe*	**sanglier/laie**	*wild boar/wild sow*
cheval/jument	*horse/mare*	**singe/guenon**	*monkey/female monkey*
coq/poule	*rooster/hen*	**taureau/vache**	*bull/cow*

Épicène

Most names of animals are **épicène**. This strange-sounding word comes from the Greek *epikoinos*, meaning "common." **Épicène** nouns work with either gender. To differentiate between the two sexes, you add **mâle** or **femelle**. Here are some masculine names:

aigle	*eagle*	**faucon**	*falcon*	**mille-pattes**	*millipede*
blaireau	*badger*	**gorille**	*gorilla*	**oiseau**	*bird*
brochet	*pike*	**guépard**	*cheetah*	**panda**	*panda*
cachalot	*sperm whale*	**hanneton**	*cockchafer*	**papillon**	*butterfly*
canari	*canary*	**hibou**	*owl*	**perroquet**	*parrot*
castor	*beaver*	**hippocampe**	*sea horse*	**phoque**	*seal*
cochon	*pig*	**hippopotame**	*hippopotamus*	**pigeon**	*pigeon*
corbeau	*crow*	**homard**	*lobster*	**pingouin**	*penguin*
crapaud	*toad*	**jaguar**	*jaguar*	**requin**	*shark*
crocodile	*crocodile*	**kangourou**	*kangaroo*	**rhinocéros**	*rhinoceros*
cygne	*swan*	**koala**	*koala*	**saumon**	*salmon*
dauphin	*dolphin*	**lama**	*llama*	**scorpion**	*scorpion*
dromadaire	*dromedary*	**léopard**	*leopard*	**serpent**	*snake*
écureuil	*squirrel*	**lézard**	*lizard*	**vautour**	*vulture*
escargot	*snail*	**lynx**	*lynx*	**zèbre**	*zebra*

Here are some feminine names:

abeille	*bee*	**girafe**	*giraffe*	**mouche**	*fly*
autruche	*ostrich*	**grenouille**	*frog*	**mouette**	*gull*
baleine	*whale*	**grive**	*thrush*	**panthère**	*panther*
chauve-souris	*bat*	**guêpe**	*wasp*	**perruche**	*budgie*
chouette	*owl*	**hirondelle**	*swallow*	**pie**	*magpie*
cigale	*cicada*	**huître**	*oyster*	**souris**	*mouse*
cigogne	*stork*	**libellule**	*dragonfly*	**taupe**	*mole*
colombe	*dove*	**loutre**	*otter*	**tortue**	*turtle*
crevette	*shrimp*	**mante religieuse**	*manta ray*	**tourterelle**	*turtledove*
fourmi	*ant*	**marmotte**	*woodchuck*	**truite**	*trout*
gazelle	*gazelle*	**méduse**	*jellyfish*	**vipère**	*viper*

Flaubert a emprunté **un perroquet** empaillé au musée de Rouen et l'a placé sur son bureau.	*Flaubert borrowed **a stuffed parrot** from the Rouen Museum and placed it on his desk.*
Tu commandes **le homard** ou **des huîtres**?	*Are you ordering **lobster** or **oysters**?*

Compléter avec l'article défini *le* ou *la*.

1. _____ vache est agacée par _____ mouche qui tourne autour de sa tête.

2. En théorie, _____ lièvre court plus vite que _____ tortue.

3. _____ perroquet de _____ tante de Xavier répète sans cesse les mêmes mots.

4. Je veux choisir _____ chameau qui me plaît pour faire un tour dans le désert.

5. _____ louve et _____ ourse protègent farouchement leurs petits.

6. _____ cigale chante pendant que _____ fourmi travaille.

7. LÉO, _____ chat de Mademoiselle Gallatin est un magnifique Maine Coon.

8. _____ oiseau qui se perche sur notre balcon est un rouge-gorge.

9. As-tu mangé _____ saumon que tu as attrapé?

10. _____ guêpe qui était sur la table a fini par la piquer.

EXERCICE
2·6

Indiquer le mâle qui correspond aux animaux ci-dessous.

1. la chamelle _____

2. la chèvre _____

3. la truie _____

4. la louve _____

5. l'oie _____

6. la chevrette _____

7. la jument _____

8. l'agnelle _____

9. la biche _____

10. la brebis _____

Across the universe

Places and the calendar

No, geography is not neutral either. There are rules—and exceptions. Let's start with cities.

Cities

The masculine is used more commonly for cities, but the feminine is still used in a more aesthetic or romantic sense. There is no set rule. You will find many examples in literature. Look at the following examples:

Le Paris populaire des années 1930	*The working-class **Paris** of the 1930s*
Paris est si **bruyant**; c'est **épuisant**.	*Paris is so **noisy**; it's **exhausting**.*
Paris, la magnifique	*Paris the magnificent*
Paris, traversée de fragrances **enivrantes**	*Paris, bathed in intoxicating fragrances*
Le Tout-Paris était **présent** pour l'inauguration du nouveau musée.	*Everybody who is anybody in Paris attended the inauguration of the new museum.*
Tout Venise souffrait des inondations.	*All of Venice suffered from the floods.*
Venise La Sérénissime	*Venice the Most Serene*
Venise, la belle, l'enchanteresse	*Venice, the beautiful, the bewitching*

Names of towns preceded by a masculine definite article are masculine:

Le Havre est **un grand port**.	*Le Havre is a big harbor.*
Le Caire est **connu** pour son musée de l'Antiquité Égyptienne.	*Cairo is known for its museum of Egyptian antiquity.*
Le Mans est **connu** pour sa course automobile.	*Le Mans is known for its car racing.*

Names of towns preceded by a feminine definite article are feminine:

La Rochelle est très **prisée** par les vacanciers.	*La Rochelle is highly **rated** by vacationers.*
La Havane est **fréquentée** par de merveilleux musiciens.	*Marvelous musicians are to be **found** in **Havana**.*
La Seyne-sur-Mer est **située** dans le Var.	*La Seyne-sur-Mer is **in** the Var.*

The gender of Italian cities varies:

La Florence des Médicis
Le Florence de James Ivory (in *Room with a View*)
La Venise de Casanova
Le Venise de Pasolini

It all depends on the context.

Usually, when the nouns of cities are preceded by the adjectives **grand**, **nouveau**, and **vieux**, they are used in the masculine form:

Le Grand Prague	**Le Vieux-Marseille**
Le Nouveau-Belleville	**Le Vieux-Québec**

Departments, regions, and states

Now we are going to travel around the provinces and departments of France and states of America and try to figure out their genders.

Departments

Many departments take the gender of a river, a mountain, or a geographic site, like the coast.

l'Auvergne	**la Dordogne**	**la Loire**
le Cantal	**le Finistère**	**la Manche**

Le tunnel sous **la Manche** est ouvert depuis 1994.	*The Chunnel has been open since 1994.*
Dans **le Finistère**, Concarneau, ville médiévale entourée de remparts, attire de nombreux touristes.	*In **the Finistère**, Concarneau, a medieval walled town, attracts many tourists.*

Some departments are named after two rivers. If one river is masculine, it goes first and the noun is masculine. If both are feminine, the department is feminine.

l'Ille-et-Vilaine	le Maine-et-Loire	la Saône-et-Loire
l'Indre-et-Loire	la Meurthe-et-Moselle	le Tarn-et-Garonne
le Loir-et-Cher		

Chenonceau est l'un des plus beaux châteaux de **l'Indre-et-Loire**.	*Chenonceau is one of the most beautiful castles in **Indre-et-Loire**.*
La Meurthe-et-Moselle a l'une des productions les plus élevécs de mirabelles de France.	*La **Meurthe-et-Moselle** has one of the highest productions of mirabelle plums in France.*

Some departments are classified according to geographic parameters:

les Bouches-du-Rhône	les Hauts-de-Seine	la Seine-Saint-Denis
les Côtes-d'Armor	le Puy-de-Dôme	le Val-de-Marne
la Côte-d'Or		

Le Puy-de-Dôme porte le nom du volcan endormi en Auvergne.	*Le **Puy-de-Dôme** bears the name of the dormant volcano in Auvergne.*
La Seine-Saint-Denis est le 93ème département français. On l'appelle 9-3.	*La **Seine-Saint-Denis** is the 93rd French department. It is called 9-3.*

Others are determined by an adjective. Departments ending in **-e** tend to be feminine.

| les Alpes-Maritimes | la Haute-Loire | la Haute-Vienne |
| le Bas-Rhin | la Haute-Savoie | les Pyrénées-Atlantiques |

Le lac d'Annecy **en Haute-Savoie** est l'un des plus grands de France.	*The Annecy Lake **in Haute-Savoie** is one of the largest in France.*
Le festival du cinéma a lieu à Cannes dans **les Alpes-Maritimes**.	*The film festival takes place in Cannes in the **Alpes-Maritimes**.*

Many nouns of departments that do not end in **-e** tend to be masculine:

l'Ain	le Cantal	le Gers	le Loiret
l'Allier	le Cher	l'Hérault	le Nord
l'Aveyron	le Gard	le Jura	le Tarn
le Calvados			

L'Enfant sauvage de Truffaut est basé sur une histoire vraie dans **l'Aveyron** du dix huitième siècle.	The Wild Child *by Truffaut is based on a true story in the eighteenth-century **Aveyron** department.*
Le pont du **Gard** est un aqueduc romain qui enjambe le Gard.	*The Pont du **Gard** is a Roman aqueduct that crosses the Gard river.*

The overseas departments, called **les départements ultramarins**, are:

la Guadeloupe	la Martinique	la Réunion
la Guyane	Mayotte	

There are many ultramarine territories and collectives like:

la Nouvelle-Calédonie	Saint-Pierre et Miquelon
la Polynésie	les Terres Australes et Antarctiques

Le plus grand poète de **la Martinique** fut Aimé Césaire.	*The greatest poet in **Martinique** was Aimé Césaire.*
Mayotte est devenu le 101ème département français en mars 2011.	*As of March 2011, **Mayotte** has become the 101st French Department.*

If you are interested in the topic, visit the government website on the ultramarine departments and collectives: http://www.outre-mer.gouv.fr.

Regions and states

Regions, provinces, and states ending in **-e** tend to be feminine. The others tend to be masculine—with some exceptions, of course. Here are some examples in the masculine in France:

le Bordelais	le Languedoc	le Midi	le Poitou
le Jura	le Limousin	le Nord-Pas-de-Calais	le Roussillon

Les châteaux cathares **du Languedoc** sont remplis de mystère.	*The Cathar castles **in Languedoc** are full of mystery.*
La capitale **du Poitou** est Poitiers.	*The capital **of Poitou** is Poitiers.*

Here are some examples in the feminine in France:

l'Alsace	la Bretagne	la Franche-Comté	la Picardie
l'Aquitaine	la Champagne	la Lorraine	la Provence
l'Auvergne	la Côte d'Azur	la Normandie	la Savoie
la Bourgogne			

Un des personnages les plus célèbres **d'Aquitaine** est Aliénor d'Aquitaine qui fut reine de France puis d'Angleterre.	*One of most famous figures **of Aquitaine** was Eleanor of Aquitaine who was queen of France, then of England.*
La Picardie est composée de trois départements: l'Aisne, l'Oise et la Somme.	*The **Picardy region** is composed of three departments: l'Aisne, l'Oise, and la Somme.*

Here are some examples in the masculine in the United States:

le Colorado	le Minnesota	le New-Hampshire	le Texas
le Kansas	le Mississippi	le Nouveau-Mexique	le Vermont
le Maine	le Nebraska	l'Ohio	le Wyoming
le Michigan			

Here are some examples in the feminine in the United States:

la Californie	la Floride	la Louisiane	la Virginie
la Caroline-du-Sud	la Géorgie	la Pennsylvanie	

La Californie est l'un des États les plus visités par les Européens.
California is one of the states most visited by Europeans.
Napoléon vendit la Louisiane en 1803.
Napoleon sold Louisiana in 1803.

Note that you will say **l'État de New York** to avoid the confusion between New York State and New York City and **l'État de Washington** to distinguish between the state of Washington and Washington, D.C., the capital of the country. There are quite a few tricks to be aware of, so double-check the article and the preposition in the dictionary.

EXERCICE

3·1

Indiquer le genre des noms en ajoutant l'article défini _le_, _la_ ou _les_.

1. _____ Californie

2. _____ Seine-Saint-Denis

3. _____ Louisiane

4. _____ Bretagne

5. _____ Guadeloupe

6. _____ Caire

7. _____ Languedoc

8. _____ Dordogne

9. _____ Nebraska

10. _____ Vermont

11. _____ Maine

12. _____ Lorraine

13. _____ New Jersey

14. _____ Limousin

15. _____ Gard

16. _____ Poitou

17. _____ Missouri

18. _____ Provence

19. _____ Martinique

20. _____ Alpes-Maritimes

Countries

Like regions and states, the countries with an **-e** ending tend to be feminine. Other endings tend to be masculine, although you must watch out for the exceptions.

First, let's look at the feminine countries:

l'Albanie	*Albania*	la Hongrie	*Hungary*
l'Algérie	*Algeria*	l'Inde	*India*
l'Allemagne	*Germany*	l'Irlande	*Ireland*
l'Angleterre	*England*	l'Italie	*Italy*
l'Arabie saoudite	*Saudi Arabia*	la Jordanie	*Jordan*
l'Argentine	*Argentina*	la Malaisie	*Malaysia*
l'Australie	*Australia*	la Mauritanie	*Mauritania*
l'Autriche	*Austria*	la Mongolie	*Mongolia*
la Belgique	*Belgium*	la Namibie	*Namibia*
la Biélorussie	*Belarus*	la Norvège	*Norway*
la Bolivie	*Bolivia*	la Pologne	*Poland*
la Bulgarie	*Bulgaria*	la Roumanie	*Romania*
la Chine	*China*	la Russie	*Russia*
la Colombie	*Columbia*	la Suède	*Sweden*
la Côte d'Ivoire	*Ivory Coast*	la Syrie	*Syria*
l'Égypte	*Egypt*	la Tanzanie	*Tanzania*
l'Espagne	*Spain*	la Thaïlande	*Thailand*
l'Éthiopie	*Ethiopia*	la Tunisie	*Tunisia*
la Finlande	*Finland*	la Turquie	*Turkey*
la France	*France*	la Sierra Leone	*Sierra Leone*
la Grèce	*Greece*	l'Ukraine	*Ukraine*
la Guyane	*Guyana*	la Zambie	*Zambia*

Here are some exceptions. The following nouns end with an **-e** but are masculine:

le Cachemire	*Kashmir*	le Mozambique*	*Mozambique*
le Cambodge	*Cambodia*	le Zimbabwe**	*Zimbabwe*
le Mexique	*Mexico*		

*officially **la République du Mozambique**
or **la République du Zimbabwe

La Suède attribue les prix Nobel chaque année.	***Sweden*** *awards Nobel prizes every year.*
Attiré par Istanbul, son frère s'est installé **en Turquie** l'an passé.	*Attracted by Istanbul, his brother settled **in Turkey** last year.*

Now let's look at some of the masculine countries:

l'Afghanistan	*Afghanistan*	le Kenya	*Kenya*
le Bangladesh	*Bangladesh*	le Laos	*Laos*

le Bénin	*Benin*	**le Liban**	*Lebanon*
le Bhoutan	*Bhutan*	**le Maroc**	*Morocco*
le Brésil	*Brazil*	**le Mali**	*Mali*
le Canada	*Canada*	**le Nigéria**	*Nigeria*
le Chili	*Chile*	**le Pakistan**	*Pakistan*
le Congo	*Congo*	**le Paraguay**	*Paraguay*
le Danemark	*Denmark*	**le Pérou**	*Peru*
l'Équateur	*Ecuador*	**le Portugal**	*Portugal*
le Gabon	*Gabon*	**le Sénégal**	*Senegal*
l'Iran	*Iran*	**le Tchad**	*Chad*
l'Irak	*Iraq*	**le Venezuela**	*Venezuela*
le Japon	*Japan*	**le Viêt-Nam**	*Vietnam*

Some countries do not have articles: **Israël, Oman.**

Le Viêt-Nam est l'un des plus grands producteurs de riz.	*Vietnam is one of the largest rice producers.*
Le Maroc a de nombreux sites protégés par l'UNESCO.	*Morocco has many sites protected by UNESCO.*

EXERCICE
3·2

Indiquer le genre des noms en ajoutant l'article défini *le*, *la* ou *les*.

1. _____ France

2. _____ Danemark

3. _____ Grèce

4. _____ Mexique

5. _____ Belgique

6. _____ Japon

7. _____ Chili

8. _____ Guatemala

9. _____ Brésil

10. _____ Cambodge

11. _____ Italie

12. _____ Portugal

13. _____ Chine

14. _____ Turquie

15. _____ Russie

16. _____ Bolivie

17. _____ Malaisie

18. _____ Nouvelle-Calédonie

19. _____ Costa Rica

20. _____ Philippines

EXERCICE

3·3

Indiquer le genre des pays ou provinces en ajoutant l'article défini _le_ ou _la_.

1. _____ Népal est un endroit idéal pour le trekking.

2. _____ Jordanie abrite l'ancienne cité de Pétra, patrimoine mondial de l'UNESCO.

3. En mars, Erwan visitera _____ Togo, _____ Bénin et _____ Sierra Leone.

4. _____ Nouvelle-Zélande attire Carla depuis longtemps.

5. _____ Guyane est un département ultramarin.

6. _____ Burkina Faso organise un gigantesque festival de cinéma tous les deux ans.

7. _____ Qatar a invité des architectes français pour construire des édifices.

8. _____ Viêt-Nam a fortement influencé l'écriture de Marguerite Duras.

9. _____ Pays-Bas sont de grands exportateurs de tulipes.

10. _____ Québec est traversé par le Saint-Laurent.

Islands, rivers, seas, and oceans

Now we are going to investigate the gender of islands and rivers. Could there be set rules?

Islands

The rules for the gender of isles are as fluctuant as their waters. You will find variations from one dictionary to the other, from one writer to the other. It remains a poetic enigma of islands . . . Even if the island is a state, the tendency is to use the feminine, referring to **l'île**, but not always. In fact, some islands do not even have articles:

Aruba	**Guernesey**	**Jersey**	**Samoa**
Bora, Bora	**Haïti**	**Madagascar**	**Terre-Neuve**
Chypre	**Hawaï**	**Malte**	**Taïwan**
Cuba	**Hong-Kong**	**Ouessant**	

Madagascar est situé dans l'océan Indien.		*Madagascar is in* the Indian Ocean.	
Haïti chérie		*Darling Haiti* (political song, 1920)	
Cuba, la belle		*Cuba, the beautiful*	
Au quinzième siècle, **Cuba était peuplée** par les Taïnos.		*In the fifteenth century,* ***Cuba was inhabited*** *by the Taino Indians.*	
Taïwan est située au centre de l'Asie.		*Taiwan is in* the center of Asia.	

Some islands have a definite article, making things easy:

la Barbade	la Grenade	l'Île de Sein	les Marquises
le Cap-Vert	la Guadeloupe	la Jamaïque	la Nouvelle-Guinée
la Corse	l'Île Maurice	les Maldives	les Seychelles
la Crête	l'Île de Ré	la Martinique	la Sicile

La Corse est renommée pour **ses falaises**.   *Corsica is renowned for* ***its cliffs***.
L'Île de Ré est l'île **favorite** des politiques français.   *The island of Ré is the* ***favorite*** *island of French politicians.*
Jacques Brel a passé de longues années **aux enchanteresses Marquises**.   *Jacques Brel spent many years on the* ***enchanting Marquesas Islands***.

Rivers

In French, there is a difference between **un fleuve**, a river that flows into the sea or the ocean, and **une rivière**, which does not. Most **fleuves** not ending with **-e** are masculine. Watch out for exceptions! Here are a few examples from around the world:

Feminine			
l'Amazone	la Krishnâ	la Seine	la Volga
la Garonne	la Loire	la Vistule	

Masculine			
le Colorado	le Mékong	le Rhin	la Tamise
le Congo	le Mississippi	le Rhône	le Tibre
le Danube	le Missouri	le Rio Grande	le Yangzy Jiang
le Gange	le Niger	le Saint-Laurent	le Yukon
l'Hudson	le Nil	le Sénégal	le Zambèze

Le Mississippi est le plus long fleuve des États-Unis.   *The Mississipi is the longest river in the United States.*
Le Gange est le fleuve sacré de l'Inde.   *The Ganges is the sacred river of India.*

Les rivières are either masculine or feminine. Here are a few examples in France:

le Cher	le Doubs	le Gers	la Mayenne
la Creuse	la Drôme	le Loir	la Moselle
la Dordogne	le Gard	le Lot	

La Dordogne est une rivière serpentine de presque 500 kilomètres.	*The Dordogne is a serpentine river almost 500 kilometers long.*
Le château de Chenonceau est construit sur un pont qui enjambe **le Cher.**	*The Chenonceau castle is built on a bridge across **the river Cher.***

EXERCICE

3·4

Indiquer le genre des noms des rivières et des fleuves en ajoutant l'article défini *le* ou *la*.

1. _____ Rio Grande

2. _____ Somme

3. _____ Mékong

4. _____ Volga

5. _____ Loire

6. _____ Mississippi

7. _____ Têt

8. _____ Drâ

9. _____ Niger

10. _____ Rance

11. _____ Potomac

12. _____ Tumen

13. _____ Loir

14. _____ Seine

15. _____ Pô

16. _____ Drôme

17. _____ Nil

18. _____ Rhône

19. _____ Dordogne

20. _____ Vienne

Seas and oceans

La mer (*sea*) is feminine and **l'océan** (*ocean*) is masculine; that is fairly easy. The common mistakes have to do with capitalization. Always check in the dictionary.

le golfe de Californie	*the Gulf of California*	**la mer Noire**	*the Black Sea*
		la mer du Nord	*the North Sea*
le golfe du Mexique	*the Gulf of Mexico*	**l'océan Atlantique**	*the Atlantic Ocean*
le golfe Persique	*the Persian Gulf*	**l'océan Indien**	*the Indian Ocean*
la mer des Caraïbes	*the Caribbean Sea*	**l'océan Pacifique**	*the Pacific Ocean*
la mer de Chine	*the China Sea*		

L'Île Maurice, territoire ultramarin de la France, se trouve dans **l'océan Indien**. Éric Tabarly a fait la traversée de **l'océan Atlantique** bien des fois.

*Mauritius Island, ultramarine territory of France is in **the Indian Ocean**. Éric Tabarly crossed **the Atlantic Ocean** many times.*

Days, months, seasons, cardinal points

The days of the week are masculine:

le lundi	*Monday*
le mardi	*Tuesday*
le mercredi	*Wednesday*
le jeudi	*Thursday*
le vendredi	*Friday*
le samedi	*Saturday*
le dimanche	*Sunday*

The months of the year are also masculine:

janvier	*January*
février	*February*
mars	*March*
avril	*April*
mai	*May*
juin	*June*
juillet	*July*
août	*August*
septembre	*September*
octobre	*October*
novembre	*November*
décembre	*December*
un avril ensoleillé	*a sunny April*
un septembre venté	*a windy September*

The seasons are masculine:

un hiver froid	*a cold winter*
un printemps tardif	*a late spring*
un été pourri	*a rotten summer*
un automne pluvieux	*a rainy fall*

Cardinal points are also masculine:

le nord	*north*
le sud	*south*
l'est	*east*
l'ouest	*west*

Religious celebrations and holidays

Noël is usually used in the masculine form and without an article:

Nous serons chez notre grand-mère à **Noël**.	*We'll be at our grandmother's for **Christmas**.*

However, you may find an article when the day is qualified:

Nous avons eu **un Noël** sous la neige.	*We had **a snowy Christmas**.*

Do not be surprised if you find articles in front of the noun in old tales and literature:

Voici **la Noël** qui arrive.	***Christmas** is coming.*

Some other holiday-related terms to keep in mind:

- **Pâque** used in the singular means *Passover*.
- **La Pâque orthodoxe** means *Orthodox Easter*.
- **Pâques** in the plural means *Easter*.
- **L'Ascension** (*Ascension Day*), **la Pentecôte** (*Pentecost*), and **la Toussaint** (*All Saints' Day*) are all feminine.
- **Le Ramadan** and **l'Aïd al Kébir** are masculine.
- **Thanksgiving** is masculine.

Now, let's see how to send holiday greetings:

Je vous souhaite...	*I wish you . . .*
...un Joyeux Noël	*. . . Merry Christmas*
...un bon Ramadan	*. . . Happy and Blessed Ramadan*
...un joyeux Thanksgiving	*. . . Happy Thanksgiving*
...de joyeuses Pâques	*. . . Happy Easter*
...une bonne et heureuse année	*. . . Happy New Year*
...une bonne année du singe	*. . . Happy Year of the Monkey*

Indiquer le genre des noms en ajoutant l'article défini *le* ou *la*.

_____ automne prochain, j'irai à l'Île Maurice dans _____ océan Indien. L'Île

Maurice est merveilleuse car c'est une île volcanique. Puis _____ été suivant, mon

amie Anne et moi envisageons de faire une croisière en Norvège. Anne connaît _____

mer Noire et _____ golfe du Mexique. En raison du travail de ses parents, elle a

beaucoup voyagé. Elle rêve de voir _____ océan Pacifique. Nous irons sans doute

ensemble un de ces jours.

Strawberry fields forever

Plants, wine, and cheese

We are going explore the world of flowers, trees, and bushes and see if we can figure out a rule.

Flowers, tree, shrubs

Let's start with flowers. They play an important role in French life and also in art, especially in painting.

Flowers

One could think that flowers are feminine since flowers are delicate and feminine. That would be not only politically incorrect but also totally wrong. The truth is that most flowers not ending in -**e** tend to be masculine.

> Hint: Try memorizing the gender of some flowers and connecting them with a person you know: Jérôme/**le tournesol**, Marie/**l'aubépine**, and so on.

Here are flowers with a masculine gender:

l'arum	*arum lily*	**le glaïeul**	*gladiola*
l'aster	*aster*	**l'hortensia**	*hydrangea*
le bégonia	*begonia*	**l'iris**	*iris*
le bouton d'or	*buttercup*	**le jasmin**	*jasmine*
le cactus	*cactus*	**le myosotis**	*forget-me-not*
le camélia	*camellia*	**le narcisse**	*narcissus*
le chrysanthème	*chrysanthemum*	**le nénuphar**	*water lily*
le coquelicot	*poppy*	**le nymphéa**	*white water lily (Monet)*
le cyclamen	*cyclamen*		
le freesia	*freesia*	**l'œillet**	*carnation*
le géranium	*geranium*	**le tournesol**	*sunflower*

Here are flowers with a feminine gender. Note that they all end with -e:

l'anémone	anemone	la pivoine	peony
l'angélique	angelica	la primevère	primrose
la capucine	nasturtium	la rose	rose
la colchique	autumn crocus	la rue	rue
la jacinthe	hyacinth	la rose d'Inde	African marigold
la jonquille	daffodil	la rose pompon	button rose
la marguerite	daisy	la rose trémière	hollyhock
l'orchidée	orchid	la tulipe	tulip
la patience	patience dock	la véronique	speedwell/veronica
la pensée	pansy	la violette	violet

Elle effeuillait **la marguerite**.

*She was playing "**he loves me, he loves me not**."*

Le tournesol était une des fleurs favorites de Van Gogh.

The sunflower was one of Van Gogh's favorite flowers.

Trees and shrubs

Most trees and shrubs tend to be masculine:

l'abricotier	apricot tree	l'érable	maple	le palmier	palm tree
l'acacia	acacia	l'eucalyptus	eucalyptus	le pêcher	peach tree
l'acajou	mahogany	le figuier	fig tree	le peuplier	poplar tree
l'aulne	alder	le frangipanier	frangipani tree	le pin	pine
le bananier	banana tree	le genévrier	juniper	le platane	plane tree
le bambou	bamboo	le groseillier	currant bush	le poirier	pear tree
le bouleau	birch	le hêtre	beech tree	le pommier	apple tree
le cèdre	cedar	l'hévéa	hevea	le prunier	plum tree
le cerisier	cherry tree	le houx	holly	le rhododendron	rhododendron
le charme	hornbeam	le laurier	laurel	le rosier	rosebush
le châtaignier	chestnut tree	le lilas	lilac tree	le sapin	fir tree
le chêne	oak	le marronnier	chestnut tree	le saule	willow
le chèvrefeuille	honeysuckle	le mélèze	larch	le séquoia	sequoia
le citronnier	lemon tree	l'olivier	olive tree	le tilleul	lime tree
le cocotier	coconut palm	l'orme	elm tree	le tremble	aspen
le cyprès	cypress				

Here are a few exceptions:

l'aubépine	hawthorn	la ronce	bramble
la bruyère	heather	la vigne	vine

En France, de nombreuses routes sont bordées de **marronniers**.	In France, many roads are lined with **chestnut trees**.
Le bambou est très utilisé dans le décor moderne.	*Bamboo is used a lot in modern décor.*

EXERCICE 4·1

Compléter avec l'article défini ou indéfini *un, une, le* ou *la* selon le sens.

1. Dans le jardin de Victoire, il y a _____ lilas et _____ laurier rose.

2. _____ rose sur ton chapeau est fanée.

3. Nous étions à la campagne et il a cueilli _____ bouton d'or.

4. Quand il était jeune, Bernard est tombé sur _____ cactus.

5. _____ chrysanthème est l'emblème national du Japon.

6. La mariée tenait _____ orchidée de la main gauche.

7. _____ séquoia que j'ai pris en photo faisait huit mètres de diamètre.

8. L'automobiliste s'est écrasé contre _____ platane.

9. Sur chaque table du restaurant, il y avait _____ rose rouge dans un vase noir.

10. _____ chêne dans le jardin de mon grand-père a près de 150 ans.

EXERCICE 4·2

Ajouter l'article défini *le* ou *la*.

1. _____ pivoine rose signifie la sincérité. Vous pouvez compter sur moi.

2. _____ tournesol signifie que vous êtes mon soleil; je ne vois que vous.

3. _____ pensée signifie que je ne veux pas que vous m'oubliiez.

4. _____ mimosa signifie que je doute de votre amour.

5. _____ jacinthe signifie que je suis conscient de votre beauté.

6. _____ bégonia signifie que mon amitié pour vous est sincère.

7. _____ véronique signifie fidélité, âme sœur.

8. _____ bouton d'or signifie que vous vous moquez de moi.

9. _____ narcisse signifie l'égoïsme.

10. _____ rue signifie que j'aime l'indépendance.

Les fleurs ont leur langage. Check online sites for the meanings of flowers, and you will find quite a few versions of their significance. But never offer a chrysanthemum, as it is related to death. You will see them in the cemeteries **à la Toussaint**.

Fruit and vegetables

The names of fruit, nuts, and vegetables not ending in -e are usually masculine:

l'abricot	*apricot*	**le coing**	*quince*	**le navet**	*turnip*
l'ail	*garlic*	**le cornichon**	*gherkin*	**l'oignon**	*onion*
l'ananas	*pineapple*	**le cresson**	*cress*	**le piment**	*chili, pepper*
l'artichaut	*artichoke*	**l'épinard**	*spinach*	**le poireau**	*leek*
l'avocat	*avocado*	**le fenouil**	*fennel*	**le petit pois**	*garden pea*
le brocoli	*broccoli*	**le haricot**	*bean*	**le pois chiche**	*chickpea*
le brugnon	*white nectarine*	**le kiwi**	*kiwi*	**le poivron**	*sweet pepper*
le cassis	*black currant*	**le litchi**	*litchi*	**le potiron**	*pumpkin*
le céleri	*celery*	**le maïs**	*corn*	**le pruneau**	*prune*
le champignon	*mushroom*	**le manioc**	*manioc*	**le quinoa**	*quinoa*
le chou	*cabbage*	**le marron**	*chestnut*	**le radis**	*radish*
le chou-fleur	*cauliflower*	**le melon**	*melon*	**le raisin**	*grapes*
le citron	*lemon*				

Here are a few exceptions:

le concombre	*cucumber*	**le gingembre**	*ginger*	**le pamplemousse**	*grapefruit*

Here are some feminine nouns of fruit, nuts, and vegetables:

l'airelle	*cranberry*	**la courge**	*squash*	**l'olive**	*olive*
l'amande	*almond*	**la courgette**	*zucchini*	**l'orange**	*orange*
l'asperge	*asparagus*	**la datte**	*date*	**la pastèque**	*watermelon*

l'arachide	*peanut*	l'échalote	*shallot*	la patate douce	*sweet potato*
l'aubergine	*eggplant*	l'endive	*chicory*	la pêche	*peach*
la betterave	*beet*	la fraise	*strawberry*	la pistache	*pistachio*
la cacahouète	*peanut*	la framboise	*raspberry*	la poire	*pear*
la carotte	*carrot*	la frisée	*curly endive*	la pomme	*apple*
la châtaigne	*chestnut*	la laitue	*lettuce*	la pomme de terre	*potato*
la cerise	*cherry*	la mirabelle	*mirabelle*	la prune	*plum*
la ciboulette	*chives*	la myrtille	*blueberry*	la tomate	*tomato*
la citrouille	*pumpkin*	la noisette	*hazelnut*	la truffe	*truffle*
la clémentine	*clementine*	la noix	*nut*		

La glace à **la pistache** de chez Berthillon est la meilleure.

*Berthillon's **pistachio** ice cream is the best.*

Le citron est bon pour la peau.

Lemon is good for your skin.

EXERCICE
4·3

Compléter en ajoutant l'article indéfini *un* ou *une*.

C'est le vingtième anniversaire de Chloé. Sa cousine Lucie a invité une vingtaine de personnes. Chloé est végétarienne alors Lucie a fait un énorme gâteau et l'a décoré de toutes sortes de fruits et légumes.

Lucie a mis au milieu _____ demi-kiwi, puis _____ abricot, _____ petite poire.

Ensuite, en forme de bouquet, _____ mirabelle, _____ cassis, _____ cerise, _____

myrtille, _____ framboise, _____ cassis. À chaque coin, elle a placé _____

marron et _____ cacahouète. Pour finir, elle a mis _____ truffe au chocolat pour

chaque invité tout autour du gâteau.

Wine and cheese

Names of wines and other alcoholic beverages tend to be masculine:

l'armagnac	le chablis	le madère	le rhum
le beaujolais	le champagne	le margaux	le saint-Émilion
le bordeaux	le chinon	le médoc	le sake
le bourbon	le cognac	le muscadet	le saumur

le brandy	le côtes de Duras	le pernod	le sauternes
le cabernet	le côtes de Provence	le pouilly-fuissé	le vouvray
le calvados	le gin	le rosé d'Anjou	le whisky
le bourgogne			

Here are a few feminine exceptions:

l'anisette	la bénédictine	la mirabelle
la bière	l'eau de vie	la vodka

On utilise **le rhum** pour faire du punch.	***Rum*** *is used to make punch.*
Le calvados est fait avec des pommes.	***Calvados*** *is made from apples.*

Names of cheeses also tend to be masculine:

le beaufort	le chabichou	le gorgonzola	le pont-l'évêque
le bleu d'Auvergne	le chaumes	le gouda	le port-salut
le bleu des Causses	le cheddar	le gruyère	le raclette
le boursin	le chèvre	le livarot	le reblochon
le brie	le comté	le maroilles	le rocamadour
le brillat-savarin	le crottin de	le mascarpone	le roquefort
le brin d'amour	Chavignol	le munster	le sainte-maure
le camembert	l'emmental	le parmesan	le vacherin
le cantal	l'époisse		

La raclette goes back to the Middle Ages and was consumed by Swiss peasants who were in need of a hot meal after a long day of labor and by herders who would cook **la raclette** on a campfire. Today in France, families and especially children enjoy it in the winter. It also has become trendy in upscale restaurants that have all the proper utensils.

Raclette comes from **racler** (*to scrape*). It is served with small potatoes and Savoy wine or Pinot Gris. It is definitely not **cuisine minceur** . . .

Here are a few feminine names of cheeses:

la faisselle	la fourme	la mozzarella	la tome
la feta	la mimolette	la ricotta	

Le roquefort est le fromage idéal pour la salade d'endives.	***Roquefort*** *is the ideal cheese for endive salad.*
Achète **un chèvre** et **un camembert** au marché!	*Buy **a goat cheese** and **a camembert** at the market!*

Mettre l'article défini *un* ou *une*.

Des copains sont réunis pour une soirée vin et fromage.

—Alex, qu'est-ce que tu prends? _____ médoc et _____ beaufort?

—Non, aujourd'hui, je voudrais _____ rosé d'Anjou et _____ gorgonzola.

—Et toi, Yves?

—_____ vodka et _____ vacherin.

—_____ vodka? En quel honneur? Tu prends toujours _____ saumur!

—Oui mais demain, on part pour Moscou. Je veux m'habituer.

—D'accord, _____ vodka pour Yves et _____ chablis pour Raoul?

—Exact. _____ chablis et _____ crottin de Chavignol.

—Tout le monde est servi?

—Non, Julien, tu m'as oublié. _____ pernod et _____ chabichou.

—Désolé. Ça arrive tout de suite.

Slang

What about learning some slang? The themes of this chapter are rich in idiomatic expressions. Learning them will help you memorize the gender.

Ce film est **un navet** (turnip).	*This film is **a flop**.*
Ton oncle est **une grosse légume** chez Renault?	*Your uncle is **a big shot** at Renault?*
C'est **la fin des haricots**!	*That's **the last straw**!*
Il était rouge comme **une tomate**.	*He was as red as **a beet**.*
Arrête de raconter **des salades**!	*Stop telling **tall tales**!*
Ce journal, c'est **une feuille de chou**!	*This paper is **a rag**!*
Je n'ai plus **un radis**.	*I haven't got **a penny** to my name.*
Zoé a fait **le poireau** une demi-heure.	*Zoé was left **cooling her heels** for half an hour.*

N'oublie pas **ta banane**!	*Don't forget **your fanny pack**!*
Ça permettra **de mettre du beurre dans les épinards**.	*That'll help you **make ends meet**.*
Jean **a failli tomber dans les pommes**.	*Jean **almost fainted**.*
Il est **haut comme trois pommes**.	*He is **knee-high to a grasshopper**.*
Il a **un cœur d'artichaut**.	*He **falls in love with every girl he meets**.*
Les carottes sont cuites.	*We've **had it**!*
J'ai **la tête comme une citrouille**.	*I feel **like my head is going to explode**.*
Occupez-vous de vos oignons!	***Mind your own business**!*
Elle a **une peau de pêche**.	*She has **a peachlike complexion**.*
Ils ont **la pêche**.	*They are **in top form**.*
Il est **bonne poire**.	*He is **a real sucker**.*
Lucien est souvent **entre deux vins**.	*He is often **tipsy**.*
Elle a **le vin gai**.	*She gets **merry when she drinks**.*
Il faudra mettre **de l'eau dans ton vin**.	*You'll have **to make concessions**.*
Ce n'est pas la peine d'en faire **tout un fromage**.	*No need to make **a big fuss** about it.*

After this, I am sure a few correct genders will stick in your mind.

Like a rolling stone

Colors and fabric, the elements, cars, and brands and acronyms

One could dream that some nouns would be neutral for a change. But this is not the case, even for stones or fabric.

Colors and fabric

Let's start with the palette of colors.

Colors

The word **couleur** (*color*) is feminine, as it ends with **-eur**. The colors themselves, however, are masculine:

l'ambre	*amber*	**l'indigo**	*indigo*	**l'orange**	*orange*
l'aubergine	*aubergine*	**l'ivoire**	*ivory*	**le rose**	*pink*
le beige	*beige*	**le jaune**	*yellow*	**le rouge**	*red*
le blanc	*white*	**le kaki**	*khaki*	**le safran**	*saffron*
le bleu	*blue*	**le marron**	*brown*	**le saumon**	*salmon*
le cramoisi	*crimson*	**le noir**	*black*	**le vert**	*green*
le gris	*gray*	**l'ocre**	*ochre*	**le violet**	*violet/purple*

Le bleu de sa robe est parfaitement assorti avec **le jaune doré** de sa ceinture.	***The blue*** *of her dress coordinates perfectly with the **golden yellow** of her belt.*
Pierre, **le vert** et **le bleu**... ça ne va pas dans cette pièce!	*Pierre, **green** and **blue** . . . it does not work in this room!*

Fabric

Most names of fabric are masculine:

l'acrylique	*acrylic*	**l'écossais**	*plaid*	**l'organdi**	*organdy*
l'alpaga	*alpaca*	**le feutre**	*felt*	**le polyamide**	*polyamide*
l'angora	*angora*	**le Gore-tex**	*Gore-Tex*	**le polyester**	*polyester*

le bambou	*bamboo*	**le jacquard**	*jacquard*	**le prince**	*Prince of*
le batik	*batik*	**le jersey**	*jersey*	**de Galles**	*Wales suit*
le brocard	*brocade*	**le jute**	*jute*	**le raphia**	*raffia*
le cachemire	*cashmere*	**le lamé**	*lamé*	**le satin**	*satin*
le coton	*cotton*	**le lin**	*linen*	**le stretch**	*stretch*
le crêpe de Chine	*crêpe de Chine*	**le lycra**	*Lycra*	**le taffetas**	*taffeta*
le crêpe de soie	*silk crêpe*	**le madras**	*madras*	**le tulle**	*tulle*
le cuir	*leather*	**le mohair**	*mohair*	**le tweed**	*tweed*
le damas	*damask*	**le molleton**	*cotton fleece*	**le velours**	*velvet*
le denim	*denim*	**le nylon**	*nylon*	**le voile**	*voile*

Here are some exceptions:

la dentelle	*lace*	**la laine polaire**	*wool fleece*	**la serge**	*serge*
la flanelle	*flannel*	**la moire**	*moiré*	**la soie**	*silk*
la gabardine	*gabardine*	**la mousseline**	*muslin/ chiffon*	**la suédine**	*suedette*
la gaze	*gauze*	**la paille**	*straw*	**la viscose**	*viscose*
la laine	*wool*	**la popeline**	*poplin*		

Le pantalon de Katia est en **lin beige**. *Katia's pants are made of **beige linen**.*
Le chapeau de M. Fillon est en **paille orange**. *Mr. Fillon's hat is made of **orange straw**.*

EXERCICE
5·1

Traduire les phrases suivantes en utilisant *tu* si nécessaire.

1. One doll was wearing a pink satin dress. The other was wearing a chiffon skirt.

   _____

2. The future bride wants to wear an ivory organdie dress.

   _____

3. His daughter likes white fleece jackets.

   _____

4. I would like to give her a red cashmere scarf.

   _____

5. I love my new blue Gore-Tex gloves.

_____

6. Your angora sweater is so warm.

_____

7. The First Lady often wears a long silk dress.

_____

8. The leather your coat is made of is high quality.

_____

9. Her Lycra T-shirt is indigo.

_____

10. He always wears Prince of Wales suits.

_____

Precious and semiprecious stones

Stones can either be masculine or feminine. These are some masculine stones:

le corail	coral	**le jade**	jade	**le quartz**	quartz
le diamant	diamond	**le lapis-lazuli**	lapis lazuli	**le rubis**	ruby
le granit	granite	**le marbre**	marble	**le saphir**	sapphire
le grenat	garnet	**l'onyx**	onyx		

These are some feminine stones:

l'agate	agate	**la citrine**	citrine	**l'opale**	opal
l'aigue-marine	aquamarine	**l'émeraude**	emerald	**la topaze**	topaz
l'améthyste	amethyst	**la kunzite**	kunzite	**la tourmaline**	tourmaline
l'ardoise	slate				

Félix a offert **un rubis** à Marianne.	_Felix gave **a ruby** to Marianne._
Ce granit rose sera idéal pour notre table.	_This pink **granite** will be ideal for our table._

Metals, minerals, chemical elements

Most names of metals, minerals, and chemical elements tend to be masculine:

l'acier	steel	le cuivre	copper	l'oxygène	oxygen
l'aluminium	aluminum	l'étain	pewter	le platine	platinum
l'anthracite	anthracite	le fer	iron	le plomb	lead
l'argent	silver	le fluor	fluorine	le potassium	potassium
l'azote	nitrogen	l'hélium	helium	le plutonium	plutonium
le bronze	bronze	l'hydrogène	hydrogen	le radium	radium
le carbone	carbon	l'iode	iodine	le sel	salt
le calcium	calcium	le lithium	lithium	le soufre	sulfur
le charbon	coal	le magnesium	magnesium	le sulfite	sulfite
le chlore	chlorine	le manganèse	manganese	le titane	titanium
le chrome	chrome	le nickel	nickel	le zinc	zinc
le cobalt	cobalt	l'or	gold		

Here are a few feminine exceptions:

la bauxite	bauxite
la chaux	lime
la roche	rock

As-tu vu le film *La Ruée vers l'or*?
Il y a **du fer** dans les épinards.

Have you seen the film The **Gold** Rush?
*Spinach contains **iron**.*

EXERCICE
5·2

Indiquer le genre des noms en ajoutant l'article défini *le* ou *la*.

1. _____ émeraude

2. _____ diamant

3. _____ tourmaline

4. _____ étain

5. _____ potassium

6. _____ fer

7. _____ lithium

8. _____ marbre

9. _____ chaux

10. _____ charbon

11. _____ citrine

12. _____ quartz

13. _____ topaze

14. _____ bronze

15. _____ corail

16. _____ plomb

17. _____ bauxite

18. _____ sel

19. _____ jade

20. _____ rubis

Cars

In most cases, cars are used in the feminine form:

J'adore **ma nouvelle Citroën Picasso**.   *I love **my new Citroën Picasso**.*

However, as this list shows, some minivans or SUVs use the masculine form. It depends on the model:

la 206 (Peugeot)	**la Land Rover**	**la Panda** (Fiat)
le 4x4	**la Lexus**	**la Porsche**
la BMW	**la Mini** (BMW)	**la Renault Clio**
la Coccinelle (Beetle/Volkswagen)	**la Mondéo** (Ford)	**la Renault Scénic**
la Ferrari	**le monospace** (minivan)	**la Smart**
la Golf	**le** (ou **la**) **Kangoo**	**la Volvo familiale**
la jeep	**le Pajero** (Mitsubishi)	

Mon monospace est en panne. Peux-tu me prêter **ton Pajero**?

My minivan has broken down. Can you lend me your Mitsubishi?

Sa Volvo est parfaite pour son travail. Mais moi, je préfère **ma Coccinelle**.

His Volvo is perfect for his job. But I prefer my Beetle.

An anecdote from Quebec: In the past, a car was called **un véhicule automobile** and was little by little abbreviated to **un automobile**. The change was made in the 1940s. However, this is often described as **usage flottant** and you may hear:

Il s'est offert **un gros Chevrolet.**   *He treated himself **to a big Chevrolet.***

Instead of:

Il s'est offert **une grosse Chevrolet.**   *He treated himself **to a big Chevrolet.***

We can use some of the many slang terms to talk about cars:

In France
la bagnole	*car/wheels*	**le tacot**	*clunker*
la caisse	*car/wheels*	**un tas de ferraille**	*pile of junk*
la guimbarde	*jalopy*	**la tire**	*old rattletrap*

In Quebec
le char	*car/wheels*	**la minoune**	*clunker*

Il a pris **sa caisse** pour aller faire un tour avec sa meuf.   *He took **his wheels** to go for a ride with his girlfriend.*
On va pas descendre sur la Côte avec **ton tas de ferraille!**   *We're not going to the Riviera with **your pile of junk!***

EXERCICE
5·3

Compléter avec l'adjectif possessif *son* ou *sa*.

Le père de mon copain Luc adore _____ BMW alors que sa femme préfère _____ Mini. Luc voudrait bien avoir _____ Pajero à lui tout seul mais ses parents ne sont pas d'accord. S'il passe le bac, il pourra rendre ses copains jaloux avec _____ Smart ou _____ Coccinelle.

Brands and acronyms

Like anything else, brands and acronyms follow a rule.

Brands

Brand names take the gender of the products they represent. For example, **une poupée** (*doll*) is feminine, so *Barbie* will be **une Barbie.**

Brand name	Derivation	
le bikini	le maillot de bain	*bathing suit*
le Bic	le stylo à bille	*pen*
le Botox	le comestique	*Botox*
le Canson	le papier dessin	*drawing paper*
la cellophane	la pellicule transparente	*cellophane*
le coca	le soda	*soda*
la cocotte minute	la marmite	*pressure cooker*
le digicode	le système	*door-entry system*
l'escalator	l'escalier roulant	*escalator*
le frigidaire/frigo	le réfrigérateur	*refrigerator*
le jacuzzi	le bain bouillonnant	*Jacuzzi*
le Kärcher	le nettoyeur haute pression	*high-pressure water cleaner*
le kleenex	le mouchoir	*Kleenex*
le K-way	le coupe-vent	*windbreaker*
l'Opinel	le couteau pliable	*folding knife*
le perfecto	le blouson en cuir	*leather jacket*
le polaroïd	l'appareil photo à développement instantané	*Polaroid camera*
le Post-it	le pense-bête autocollant	*Post-It*
la poubelle	le cuve	*garbage can*
le scotch	le ruban adhésif	*Scotch tape*
le spam	le courrier électronique non sollicité	*spam*
le Stabilo	le surligneur	*highlighter*
le taser	le pistolet électrique	*Taser gun*
la Téfal	une poêle anti-adhésive	*Teflon pan*
le ou la thermos	le récipient/la bouteille isolant	*Thermos*

La poubelle was introduced in 1884 by Eugène-René Poubelle, préfet de la Seine. All owners of buildings had to provide **une poubelle** to their tenants, a measure of public hygiene.

Dorothée ne fait jamais de randonnée sans **son Opinel**.	Dorothée never goes hiking without **her Opinel knife**.
C'est à toi de descendre **la poubelle**.	It's your turn to take out **the garbage**.

The name of Casanova, the famous and talented Venetian adventurer, writer, and musician, is often used as a "brand."

Son frère Fabrice, c'est un véritable **Casanova**.	He is a real seducer.

Acronyms

Acronyms take the gender of the nouns they represent:

la BBC	la radio/la chaîne de télévision	BBC
la BD	la bande dessinée	comic strip
la CIA	l'agence	CIA
la CNN	la chaîne de télé	CNN
le FBI	le bureau	FBI
le FMI	Fonds monétaire international	IMF
le GPS	le service de positionnement par satellite	GPS
l'HLM	l'habitation à loyer modéré	public housing
le KGB	le comité	KGB
la NASA	l'administration	NASA
l'OGM	l'organisme génétiquement modifié	GMO
l'OMS	L'organisation mondiale de la Santé	WHO
l'ONG	l'organisation non gouvernementale	NGO
l'ONU	l'organisation	UN
l'OTAN	l'organisation	NATO
l'OVNI	l'objet volant non-identifié	UFO
le PACS	le pacte civil de solidarité	civil union between two people
le/la PDG	le président directeur/trice général(e)	CEO
le RER	le réseau express régional	suburban train that goes around Paris

le TGV	le train à grande vitesse	*express train*
l'UE	l'Union européenne	*EU*
l'UNESCO	l'organisation	*UNESCO*

There are also acronyms without articles, as they refer to famous people:

BB	Brigitte Bardot
VGE	Valéry Giscard d'Estaing
DSK	Dominique Strauss-Kahn
PPDA	Patrick Poivre d'Arvor

Ils ont créé **une ONG** au Brésil.	*They set up **an NGO** in Brazil.*
Tout le monde attend la decision **du FMI** sur la fraude fiscale.	*Everyone is waiting for **the IMF's** decision about tax evasion.*

EXERCICE

5·4

Traduire les phrases suivantes.

1. Pass me the salt!

_____

2. The chef always writes his menu on a slate.

_____

3. I bought some necklaces in coral and lapis lazuli in India.

_____

4. His Volvo is gray and his Clio is lemon yellow.

_____

5. The comic strip festival takes place every year in Angoulême.

_____

6. Let's go to the beach! Iodine is good for your health.

_____

7. This vase is made out of pewter.

_____

8. If real saffron were not so expensive, I would use it every day.

_____

9. My neighbor Louise saw a UFO last night in the cornfield.

_____

10. Does this TGV stop in Amiens?

_____

Speak to me

Other languages, parts of speech, and the sciences

In this chapter, we'll cover the gender of different languages, parts of speech, and also sciences. Do they have some mystery in store for us?

Names of languages

Nouns denoting particular languages are masculine. Note that, in French, the names of languages are in lowercase:

l'allemand	*German*	**le grec**	*Greek*	**le portugais**	*Portuguese*
l'anglais	*English*	**l'hindi**	*Hindi*	**le russe**	*Russian*
l'arabe	*Arabic*	**l'italien**	*Italian*	**le serbe**	*Serbian*
le bembé	*Bembe*	**le japonais**	*Japanese*	**le swahili**	*Swahili*
le chinois	*Chinese*	**le mandarin**	*Mandarin*	**le tamoul**	*Tamil*
l'espagnol	*Spanish*	**le polonais**	*Polish*	**le turc**	*Turkish*
le français	*French*				

Mai Hien a appris **le français** à Aix-en-Provence.	*Mai Hien learned **French** in Aix-en-Provence.*
Hervé a appris **le swahili** au Kenya.	*Hervé learned **Swahili** in Kenya.*

Nouns of foreign origin

Over the centuries, because of history, wars, colonialism, and the exploration of continents, the French language has absorbed words from all over the world. You will often hear that French is being contaminated by English. This is a backward approach to languages. During the Renaissance, for example, it was trendy and very chic to use Italian words in the French language. And it is a good thing, considering that French, even after borrowing words from many languages, has a much smaller vocabulary than does English, perhaps a half or a third of the English lexicon.

A large number of the nouns of foreign origin tend to be masculine. Let's look at a few examples, starting with words borrowed from English.

Nouns of English origin

Many nouns of English influence are masculine:

le baby-sitting	le camping	le flirt	le knock-out	le poker	le slogan
le badge	le cash	le footing	le know-how	le pressing	le smoking
le barman	le challenge	le freelance	le laser	le pull-over	le snack
le bermuda	le charter	le freezer	le leader	le puzzle	le snob
le best-seller	le chewing-	le gospel	le lifting	le rap	le sponsor
le blazer	gum	le hamburger	le listing	le reporter	le talkie-
le blues	le coach	le holding	le living-room	le ring	walkie (*in*
le boss	(*trainer*)	le hold-up	le lobby	(*boxing*)	*reverse*)
le boycott	le cocktail	le jackpot	(*political*)	le rock	le tank
le brainstorming	le crash	le jazz	le manager	le self-service	le thriller
le briefing	le dealer	le jean	le marketing	le shopping	le timing
le building	le fair-play	le job	l'outsider	le show	le training
le bulldozer	le fast-food	le jogging	le parking	le skateboard	le week-end
le business	le feeling	le kidnapping	le planning	le skipper	

Here are a few feminine exceptions:

la barmaid	l'overdose	la start-up
la basket	la rocking-chair	la superstar
l'interview	la snob	

Trop de **snobs** fréquentent **ce bar**.	*Too many **snobs** go to **this bar**.*
Le boss a dit que **le briefing** aurait lieu **au snack-bar**.	*The **boss** said that **the briefing** would take place **in the snackbar**.*

It would be a mistake to think that the additions of English words to the French language are a sudden occurrence. When you hear the French complaining about the invasion of the English language, do not take it too seriously. As a French person, I'm giving myself permission to say it may be more a matter of "American envy."

Foreign words have enriched the French language for centuries. The word **camping**, for instance, has been in the French dictionary since 1903 when the concept of recreational activities started to flourish before World War I.

Also be aware of the origins of English words. For example, **flirter** was borrowed from the English but actually comes from the old French **fleureter**.

The origin of the word **gadget** is uncertain. Some sources say that in the 1850s it was similar to **gâchette**, a small tool. Other sources maintain that **gadget** comes from Gaget-Gauthier, the French company that designed miniatures of the Statue of Liberty to finance Frédéric Bartholdi's project. The name *Gaget* was written on the base of the miniatures, and the Americans started calling the statue *gadget*. Then the word crossed the Atlantic again and found its place in Le Robert's dictionary in 1946 under **gadget** with the English pronunciation. And then the French created a wonderful verb: **gadgétiser**.

Some new nouns, especially those connected to technology, are added on a regular basis.

le Bluetooth	le geek	l'iPhone	le podcast	le texto	le Twitter
le buzz	l'internet	le mail	le podcasting	le tweet	le website
le chat	l'iPad	le multi-touch	le SMS		

French has borrowed from many other languages you may identify, as they are similar or close to English. If you are not sure of the meaning of a word, check your dictionary at home or any bilingual dictionary online.

Nouns of Arabic origin

The influence of the Arabic language on the French language has been significant in many fields (mathematics, alchemy, botany, astronomy, medicine, philosophy, and mysticism). The Arab army came all the way to Poitiers in the eighth century and left quite a few words behind. Arabo-Andalusian music played an important role from the ninth to the fifteenth century, spreading gradually to Provence and becoming a source of inspiration for the French troubadours. Inevitably, words traveled back and forth from Spain to France, and many words were adopted by the French. For example, who does not like to rest on a **sofa**? Until the eighteenth century, Arab architects worked their way to England and left their mark, the arabesque. In addition, about two-thirds of the names of stars come from the Arabic language, such as **Al Bali**, **Aldébaran**, **Algol**, **Almanac**, **Altaïr**, **Mizar**, **Regulus**, **Rigel**, **Sadalmelek**, **Yad**, **Zaniah**, and so on.

At least five hundred Arabic words are used in the French language on a regular basis. Another factor in play is that the second, third, and fourth generations of immigrants from Tunisia, Algeria, Morocco, Egypt, Lebanon, and so on living in France have been so creative with the language through literature and music that the count keeps going up, and the French language enriches itself.

Here are a few examples, both masculine and feminine, of words of Arabic origin:

l'alambic	l'azimut	le couscous	le harem	le magasin	le taboulé
l'alcool	le baobab	le cramoisi	le hasard	la maroquinerie	le tambour
l'algèbre	le bled	l'élixir	le henné	le matelas	le tajine

l'almanach	le camaïeu	la gazelle	la jupe	le moucharabieh	le talc
l'amalgame	le camphre	le goudron	kif-kif	le sofa	le toubib
l'ambre	le carmin	le hammam	le luth	le sumac	le zénith
l'amiral					

Nouns from other languages

The French language, over the centuries, has borrowed words from numerous other languages as well.

Nouns of Chinese origin

le feng shui	le kung-fu	le tai-chi	le yang	le wok
le ginseng	le litchi	le Tao	le yin	

Nouns of German origin

le bretzel	l'ersatz	le kitsch	le putsch
le diktat	le hamster	le leitmotiv	

Nouns of Indian origin

l'atoll	le bouddha	le karma	le yoga
l'avatar	le gourou	le nirvana	

Nouns of Italian origin

le carnaval	le farniente	le graffiti	l'opéra	la pizzeria
le chianti	le ghetto	la loggia	le piano	la polenta
le crescendo	le gnocchi	la mezzanine	la pizza	

Nouns of Japanese origin

le bonsaï	l'ikébana	le karaoké	l'origami	le sushi
la geisha	le judo	le karaté	le saké	le tofu
le haïku	le kabuki	le kimono	le samouraï	le zen
le hara-kiri	le kamikaze	le manga	le sashimi	

Nouns of Russian origin

le blini	la datcha	le morse	la toundra
le bortsch	la douma	la steppe	la vodka
le cosaque	le mammouth	la taïga	

L'amiral a commandé **une pizza** et une bouteille de **saké**.	*The admiral ordered **a pizza** with a bottle of **sake**.*
En arrivant à Marrakech, elle a mangé **un couscous** avec du thé à la menthe puis elle s'est fait teindre les cheveux au **henné**.	*Upon arriving in Marrakech, she ate **couscous** with mint tea and she **hennaed** her hair.*

Compléter avec un article défini.

1. Antoine apprend _____ japonais car il veut aussi apprendre _____ karaté.

2. _____ marketing pour _____ vodka Van Gogh a bien réussi.

3. _____ tweet a été envoyé par _____ gourou de l'ashram d'Aurobindo.

4. _____ pizza et _____ polenta qu'elle a préparées étaient délicieuses.

5. Je cherche un interprète qui parle très bien _____ chinois et _____ russe.

6. _____ Carnaval de Venise a lieu en février.

7. Dans _____ datcha, cela sentait _____ bortsch et _____ vodka.

8. Akiko, aimez-vous _____ saké? Et _____ karaoké?

9. _____ nouveau manga de Yoshihiro Togashi connaît un grand succès.

10. Ils ont chevauché dans _____ steppe de Mongolie.

Compound nouns

After memorizing the genders of single nouns, could there be a trick to figure out the gender of compound ones?

Compound nouns composed of a verb derivative and a noun

Compound nouns composed of a verb derivative and a noun tend to be masculine:

l'abat-jour	*lamp shade*	**le faire-part**	*announcement*
l'aide-mémoire	*memorandum*	**le garde-fou**	*railing, parapet,*
l'allume-gaz	*gas lighter*		*safeguard*
l'amuse-gueule	*appetizer*	**le gratte-ciel**	*skyscraper*
le brise-glace	*icebreaker*	**le lave-vaisselle**	*dishwasher*
le cache-cache	*hide and seek*	**l'ouvre-boîte**	*can opener*
le casse-noisette	*nutcracker*	**le porte-clés**	*keychain*
le chasse-neige	*snowplow*	**le porte-monnaie**	*wallet*
le coupe-vent	*windbreaker*	**le porte-savon**	*soapdish*
le croque-	*toasted ham and*	**le presse-papier**	*paper weight*
monsieur	*cheese sandwich*	**le serre-livres**	*bookends*
l'essuie-glace	*windshield wiper*	**le trompe-l'œil**	*trompe-l'œil*

One feminine exception is **la garde-robe** (*wardrobe*).

Elle vient d'acheter un **abat-jour** turquoise qui est parfait pour le vestibule.	*She just bought a turquoise **lamp shade** that is perfect for the foyer.*
Les **amuse-gueule** qu'ils ont servis étaient exquis.	*The **appetizers** they served were exquisite.*

Compound nouns composed of an adverb and a noun

Compound nouns composed of an adverb and a noun tend to take the gender of the noun. For example, **rasage** ends in **-age** so it is masculine. L'**après-rasage** is also masculine.

l'après-soleil	*after-sun lotion*	l'avant-veille	*two days before*
l'arrière-boutique	*back shop*	la mini-jupe	*mini-skirt*
l'avant-goût	*foretaste*	le sous-bois	*undergrowth, trees*
l'arrière-goût	*aftertaste*	le sous-continent	*subcontinent*
l'arrière-pensée	*ulterior motive*	le sous emploi	*underemployment*
l'arrière-plan	*background*	la sous-estimation	*underestimation*
l'avant-bras	*forearm*	le sous-marin	*submarine*
l'avant-première	*preview*	la sous-traitance	*subcontracting*

Here are a couple of exceptions: l'**avant-guerre** (*prewar years*) can be both masculine or feminine; l'**après-guerre** (*postwar years*) is only masculine.

Compound nouns composed of a noun plus a noun

Compound nouns composed of a noun and a noun tend to take the gender of the first noun:

l'appui-tête	*headrest*	l'oiseau-mouche	*hummingbird*
l'arc-en-ciel	*rainbow*	la porte-fenêtre	*French window*
le bébé-éprouvette	*test tube baby*	le portrait-robot	*identikit picture*
le drap-housse	*fitted sheet*	le soutien-gorge	*bra*
la langue-de-chat	*finger biscuit*	le timbre-poste	*postage stamp*
la main-d'œuvre	*workforce/labor*	la voiture-restaurant	*dining car*
la moissonneuse-batteuse	*combine harvester*		

Je n'ai pas trouvé de **drap-housse** assorti à ma couette.	*I have not found **the fitted sheet** that matches my duvet cover.*
Hier, nous avons vu **un** bel **arc-en-ciel** au-dessus de la mer.	*Yesterday we saw **a** beautiful **rainbow** over the sea.*

Nouns derived from verbs and adverbs

Nouns derived from verbs and adverbs tend to be masculine:

l'arrière	*back/rear*	**le derrière**	*bottom/behind*	**le manger**	*food*
l'avant	*front*	**le dessous**	*underside/back*	**le pourquoi**	*the why*
le boire	*drink*	**le dessus**	*top/right side*	**le rire**	*laugh*
le comment	*the how*	**le devant**	*front*	**le tout**	*the whole*

Tu vas t'asseoir à **l'avant** de la voiture.	*You'll sit in **the front** of the car.*
Je ne comprends pas **le pourquoi** de cette décision.	*I don't understand **why** this decision is being made.*

Abbreviated nouns

Abbreviated nouns keep the gender of the complete noun:

l'apéro/l'apéritif	*before lunch or dinner drink*	**la photo/la photographie**	*photography*
		le pseudo/le pseudonyme	*pseudonym*
le ciné/le cinéma	*cinema/movie theater*	**la radio/la radiodiffusion**	*radio*
la fac/la faculté	*school in a university, college, ability*	**le stylo/le stylographe**	*pen*
		le taxi/le taximètre	*taxi*
le métro/le métropolitain	*subway*	**la télé/la télévision**	*television*
la moto/la motocyclette	*motorbike*	**le vélo/le vélocipède**	*bicycle*
le petit dej/le petit déjeuner	*breakfast*		

Mon pseudo sur ton blog, c'est Cléopâtre.	*My pseudonym on your blog is Cleopatra.*
Et si on allait faire un tour en **vélo**?	*And what about taking **a bike** ride?*

Nouns of the sciences and academic disciplines

Names of sciences and disciplines are almost all feminine:

l'agronomie	*agronomy*	**l'électronique**	*electronics*	**la musicologie**	*musicology*
l'anatomie	*anatomy*	**la génétique**	*genetics*	**la nanoscience**	*nanoscience*
l'anthropologie	*anthropology*	**la géographie**	*geography*	**l'océanographie**	*oceanography*
l'archéologie	*archeology*	**la géologie**	*geology*	**la pédagogie**	*pedagogy*
l'astronomie	*astronomy*	**la géométrie**	*geometry*	**la philosophie**	*philosophy*
la biologie	*biology*	**l'histoire**	*history*	**la phonétique**	*phonetics*
la botanique	*botany*	**l'informatique**	*computer science*	**la physique**	*physics*

la chimie	chemistry	la linguistique	linguistics	la psychologie	psychology
la cosmologie	cosmology	la logique	logics	la sociologie	sociology
la criminologie	criminology	les mathématiques	mathematics	la spéléologie	speleology
l'écologie	ecology	la mécanique	mechanics	les statistiques	statistics
l'économie	economics	la météorologie	meteorology	la théologie	theology
l'éducation	education				

Here are a couple of masculine exceptions:

| l'art | art |
| le droit | law |

| Ma meilleure amie étudie **l'anthropologie judiciaire** à Paris. | *My best friend studies **forensic anthropology** in Paris.* |
| Laura est professeur de **linguistique** à l'Université d'Angers. | *Laura is a **linguistics** professor at the University of Angers.* |

EXERCICE
6·2

Compléter avec un article défini.

1. _____ nouvel abat-jour que tu as acheté est trop grand.

2. _____ devant de la maison a besoin de réparations.

3. Je ne peux pas trouver _____ casse-noisette. Où l'as-tu mis?

4. Thierry lui a offert _____ presse-papier en cristal dont elle rêvait.

5. Clara se demandait _____ pourquoi de toute chose.

6. Ils envisagent de construire _____ plus haut gratte-ciel du monde.

7. Quentin étudie _____ philosophie et _____ droit à la Sorbonne.

8. À quelle heure ouvre _____ voiture-restaurant?

9. _____ sous-marin *Le Redoutable* a fait une escale à Hawaï.

10. _____ lave-vaisselle est en panne. Allons au restaurant!

Traduire les phrases suivantes en utilisant *vous* si nécessaire.

1. The rainbow was red, yellow, pink, and blue.

   _____

2. Their daughter studies computer science in Paris.

   _____

3. Have you seen Sophie's wardrobe?

   _____

4. Subcontracting is a more and more common phenomenon.

   _____

5. Do you speak Spanish or Italian?

   _____

6. This country has an important foreign labor force.

   _____

7. Ginseng is good for your health.

   _____

8. The art she sells is very expensive.

   _____

9. Laurent is famous for his contagious laughter.

   _____

10. French architects will build this new skyscraper.

    _____

Anything goes

Other situations to keep in mind

Some nouns have their own idiosyncrasies: their gender varies for multiple reasons, and some are androgynous. This is just another twist to the never-ending story.

Épicène nouns: Nouns with two genders

Some nouns can be either masculine or feminine. They are call **noms épicènes**. You encountered some in Chapter 2 where, for example, **une tortue** can be either male or female.

The words that can be used with either gender are:

après-midi	*afternoon*	**oasis**	*oasis*
avant-guerre	*prewar years*	**palabres***	*never-ending discussions*
enzyme	*enzyme*	**parka**	*parka*
laque	*lacquer*	**perce-neige**	*snowdrop*
météorite	*meteorite*	**réglisse**	*liqorice*

*Used in the plural.

Arnaud a photographié **une merveilleuse oasis** couverte de palmiers dattiers.	*Arnaud photographed **a wonderful oasis** covered with date palms.*
Une météorite de 150 kg est tombée dans un champ de blé à Ensisheim, Alsace en 1492.	*A 150-kilo **meteorite** fell in a wheatfield in Ensisheim, Alsace, in 1492.*

Nouns that are masculine in the singular and feminine in the plural

The gender of some nouns changes if an adjective follows or precedes them. We'll look at **amour**, **délice**, and **gens**. **Amour** is masculine in the common, singular usage:

L'amour fou est éternel.	***Being madly in love*** *is eternal.*
« Mais combien fait mal **un amour** qui meurt! » (Pierre Loti)	*"How **a dying love** is painful!"*

If the adjective precedes the noun when it is plural, the noun and the adjective are used in the feminine plural:

Dans son roman, il raconte **ses folles amours** avec la marquise.	*In his novel, he writes about **his mad love** for the marquise.*
Elle n'oubliera jamais **ses premières amours**.	*She'll never forget **her first romantic experiences**.*
« J'aspirais secrètement à de **belles amours**. » (Honoré de Balzac)	*"I was secretly longing for **beautiful love**."*

In the case of **délice**, it is more a matter of degree. In the masculine singular, **délice** means *joy, fun*:

Quel délice de manger ces mangues bien mûres!	***What a delight*** *to eat these very ripe mangoes!*

In the feminine plural, there is a sense of pleasure, intense transport of the mind and body:

Ils profitaient **des délices** de l'amour à Venise.	*They enjoyed **the pleasures** of love in Venice.*
Nous goûtions **les délices** de la vie.	*We enjoyed **the delights** of life.*

The noun **gens** is usually masculine plural. However, if an adjective precedes the noun, both the noun and the adjective become feminine and the meaning changes:

J'ai rencontré **des gens** très **distrayants**.	*I met very **entertaining people**.*
Ces vieilles gens vivent de très peu!	***These old people*** *live on very little!*
Quelles honnêtes gens!	***How honest these people are!***
Ce sont des **petites gens** sans ressources.	*They are **poor people** without resources.*
Leurs voisins, ce sont **des braves gens**.	*Their neighbors are **good folks**.*

However, **jeunes gens**, considered as a block, remains masculine:

De nombreux **jeunes gens** faisaient la queue devant le cinéma.	*Many **young people** were standing in line in front of the cinema.*

Homographic homonyms

A number of nouns are differentiated only by their gender. The spelling and the pronunciation are identical, but the meaning is different. It is very important to be aware of these *homographic homonyms*. Let's take an example from the hair salon:

Je voudrais **une mousse** de qualité pour ma croisière dans les îles des Caraïbes.

*I would like **a quality styling mousse** for my cruise in the Caribbean Islands.*

Versus:

Je voudrais **un mousse** de qualité pour ma croisière dans les îles des Caraïbes.

*I would like **a quality cabin boy** for my cruise in the Caribbean Islands.*

Memorize the gender of such words little by little, using them in full sentences and engraving them in your mind to keep out of trouble. Compare these masculine and feminine nouns:

Masculine		Feminine	
l'aide	aide, assistant	l'aide	assistance, help
l'aigle	eagle	l'aigle	military insignia
l'aria	worry, problem	l'aria	aria
l'aune	alder	l'aune	measure/in term
le barbe	horse	la barbe	beard
le boum	boom	la boum	party
le cache	mask, cover	la cache	cache, hiding place
le carpe	carpus	la carpe	carp
le champagne	champagne	la Champagne	Champagne region
le coche	stage coach	la coche	notch, gash, groove
le crêpe	crêpe, fabric	la crêpe	pancake, crêpe
le critique	critic	la critique	review, criticism
le garde	guard, warden	la garde	guard, custody
le gène	gene	la gêne	embarrassment
le gîte	shelter, cottage	la gîte	bed of sunken ship
le greffe	clerk's office	la greffe	transplant, graft
le laque	lacquer	la laque	hairspray, shellac
le légume	vegetable	la grosse légume	big shot, bigwig
le livre	book	la livre	pound/pound sterling
le manche	handle	la manche	sleeve
		la Manche	the English Channel
le/la manœuvre	unskilled worker	la manoeuvre	maneuver, operation
le mémoire	master's thesis	la mémoire	memory
le mode	mode, way	la mode	fashion
le moule	mold, pan	la moule	mussel
le mousse	cabin boy	la mousse	moss, foam, mousse
l'œuvre	shell of a building	l'œuvre	work, works
l'ombre	grayling	l'ombre	shade, shadow
le page	page (boy)	la page	page, episode
le parallèle	parallel	la parallèle	parallel line
le pendule	pendulum	la pendule	clock
le physique	physical appearance	la physique	physics

le platine	*platinum*	**la platine**	*deck, turntable*
le poêle	*heating stove*	**la poêle**	*frying pan*
le/la politique	*politician*	**la politique**	*politics*
le poste	*job, extension*	**la poste**	*post office*
le soi	*self, oneself*	**la soie**	*silk*
le solde	*balance of an account, sale*	**la solde**	*soldier's pay*
le somme	*nap, snooze*	**la somme**	*sum, amount*
le transat	*deckchair*	**la transat**	*transatlantic race*
le trompette	*trumpet player*	**la trompette**	*trumpet*
le vague	*vagueness*	**la vague**	*wave*
le vase	*vase*	**la vase**	*slime, mud*
le vapeur	*steamship*	**la vapeur**	*steam, vapor*
le voile	*veil*	**la voile**	*sail, sailing*

On lui a fait **une greffe** de la cornée.
Amina est contente de **son nouveau poste** chez Fauchon.

*He recieved **a corneal transplant**.*
*Amina is happy with **her new position** at Fauchon's.*

EXERCICE
7·1

Compléter avec l'article défini *le, la* ou *l'*.

1. _____ livre qu'Éric a écrit est sur _____ mode en Italie.

2. Il a marché dans _____ vase et ses chaussures sont sales.

3. _____ seul légume que mon fils accepte de manger, c'est _____ brocoli chinois.

4. Elles m'ont suggéré _____ gîte dans le Lot où elles ont séjourné l'an passé.

5. _____ crêpe a collé à _____ poêle. Elle est immangeable!

6. Tu savais que Jean s'était laissé pousser _____ barbe?

7. Voudrais-tu faire de _____ voile au large de l'Île de Ré?

8. On doit lire le roman jusqu'à _____ page 150?

9. Xavier a oublié _____ mémoire qu'il doit remettre à son professeur.

10. _____ mousse pour le bain est parfumée à la lavande.

Homophonous homonyms

Homophonous homonyms are nouns that are pronounced in the same manner but have a different spelling and meaning. Some share the same gender. Others are either masculine or feminine. Let's start with the masculine.

Masculine homophonous homonyms

l'abîme	*abyss, gulf*	**abyme**	*story within a story* (mise en abyme)		
l'autel	*altar*	**l'hôtel**	*hotel*		
le baccara	*baccarat, casino*	**le baccarat**	*Baccarat crystal*		
le ban	*applause, banns*	**le banc**	*bench*		
le brocard	*brocket (deer), gibe*	**le brocart**	*brocade*		
le cahot	*jolt, bump*	**le chaos**	*chaos*		
le cep	*vine stock*	**le cèpe**	*porcini mushroom*		
le champ	*field, domain*	**le chant**	*song*		
le cœur	*heart*	**le chœur**	*choir, chorus*		
le compte	*count, account*	**le comte**	*count (nobility)*	**le conte**	*tale, story*
le cor	*horn*	**le corps**	*body, corpse*		
le crack	*ace, wizard*	**le krach**	*financial crash*		
le dessein	*goal, intention*	**le dessin**	*drawing, pattern*		
le différent	*the different person*	**le différend**	*disagreement*		
le filtre	*filter*	**le philtre**	*love potion*		
le flan	*custard flan*	**le flanc**	*flank, side, slope*		
le fond	*back, bottom*	**le fonds**	*fund, funds, capital*	**le fonts**	*baptismal font*
le galon	*piece of braid, stripe*	**le gallon**	*gallon*		
le golf	*golf*	**le golfe**	*gulf*		
le lac	*lake*	**le laque**	*lacquer*		
le Marocain	*Moroccan man*	**le maroquin**	*Morocco leather*		
le martyr	*martyr*	**le martyre**	*martyrdom, agony*		
le péché	*sin*	**le pêcher**	*peach tree*		
le plan	*plan, map*	**le plant**	*seedling, patch*		
le point	*period, dot, point*	**le poing**	*fist*		
le rancart	*scrap, heap*	**le rancard**	*rendezvous*		
le saint	*saint*	**le sein**	*breast, womb*	**le seing**	*signature (legal)*
le saut	*jump, leap*	**le sceau**	*seal/stamp*		
le seau	*bucket*	**le sot**	*fool*		
le ver	*worm*	**le verre**	*glass*		
le vers	*verse*	**le vert**	*green*		

Ce **dessin** de Matisse a été vendu aux enchères.		This Matisse **drawing** was sold at auction.	
Leur maison est construite **à flanc** de colline.		Their house is built **on** the hill**side**.	

Feminine homophonous homonyms

Other homophonous homonyms are feminine:

l'amande	almond	l'amende	fine		
la balade	walk, drive, ride, trip	la ballade	ballad		
la cane	female duck	la canne	cane/stick		
la cession	transfer/abandon	la session	session		
la chair	flesh	la chaire	university chair	la chère	food
l'encre	ink	l'ancre	anchor		
la pause	pause, break	la pose	pose, posing		
la pensée	thought	la pensée	pansy		
la tache	spot, stain	la tâche	task		
la taule	jail	la tôle	sheet metal		
la voie	way/lane	la voix	voice		

Le capitaine a jeté **l'ancre** dans le port de Dakar.		The captain cast **the anchor** in the Dakar port.	
Jean a dû payer **une amende** de 300 euros.		Jean had to pay a 300-euro **fine**.	

Masculine and feminine homophonous homonyms

In the case of masculine and feminine homophonous homonyms, the gender and the spelling are different but the pronunciation is the same.

l'air	air/tune	l'aire	area/surface	l'ère	era
le bal	ball	la balle	ball, bullet		
le bamboula	tam-tam	la bamboula	African dance		
le bar	bar	la barre	rod, bar		
le bout	end, tip	la boue	mud		
le cerf	stag	la serre	greenhouse		
le chèvre	goat cheese	la chèvre	goat		
le col	collar, pass	la colle	glue		
le cours	course, rate	la cour	yard, the royal court, courting		
le court	tennis court	la Cour suprême	Supreme Court		

le chêne	*oak tree*	**la chaîne**	*chain, channel*		
le faîte	*crest, ridge*	**la fête**	*holiday, party*		
le faux	*forgery, falsehood*	**la faux**	*scythe*		
le foie	*liver*	**la foi**	*faith*	**la fois**	*time, occurrence*
le gaz	*gas*	**la gaze**	*gauze*		
le gril	*broiler*	**la grille**	*gate, grid, scale*		
le lit	*bed*	**la lie**	*sediment, dregs*		
le luth	*lute*	**la lutte**	*struggle, wrestling*		
le mal	*evil*	**la malle**	*trunk*		
le/la maire	*mayor*	**la mer**	*sea*	**la mère**	*mother*
le mythe	*myth*	**la mite**	*moth*		
le mort	*dead man*	**la mort**	*death*		
le mur	*wall*	**la mûre**	*blackberry*		
le pair	*peer*	**la paire**	*pair*		
le parti	*party*	**la partie**	*part, game*		
le poche	*paperback*	**la poche**	*pocket, bag*		
le pois	*pea*	**le poids**	*weight*		
le pot	*pot/jar*	**la peau**	*skin*		
le pouce	*thumb*	**la pousse**	*sprout, shoot*		
le racket	*racketeering*	**la raquette**	*racket*		
le rai	*ray*	**la raie**	*line/hair part*		
le renne	*reindeer*	**la rêne**	*rein*	**la reine**	*queen*
le repère	*landmark*	**le repaire**	*den, hideout*		
le roux	*roux, russet, redhead*	**la roue**	*wheel*		
le satyre	*satyr, maniac*	**la satire**	*satire*		
le sel	*salt*	**la selle**	*saddle*		
le sol	*ground, floor*	**la sole**	*sole*		
le tic	*tic, habit*	**la tique**	*tick*		
le tome	*tome, volume*	**la tome**	*Savoy cheese*		
le tout	*whole*	**la toux**	*cough*		
le tribut	*tribute*	**la tribu**	*tribe*		
le vice	*vice/defect*	**la vis**	*screw*		

Quels cours suis-tu cette session?
Le château nous a servi de point de **repère**.

__What courses__ are you taking this session?
We used the castle as __a landmark__.

EXERCICE 7·2

Compléter avec l'article défini _le_, _la_ ou _l'_.

1. Je n'ai pas pu enlever _____ tache de vin sur ta chemise.

2. Le maître-nageur a mis _____ drapeau rouge car _____ mer est très agitée.

3. _____ diva a perdu _____ voix au beau milieu de _____ aria.

4. Vous aurez _____ peau lisse si vous utilisez cette crème hydratante.

5. La police a trouvé _____ repaire des trafiquants de drogue.

6. Attention! _____ sole jaune est tombée sur _____ sol.

7. Je ne connais pas _____ tribu dont elle a parlé lors de sa conférence.

8. Lucie a vu _____ plus vieux chêne de sa vie dans _____ forêt de Tronçais.

9. Prépare un bon repas. Bertrand aime _____ bonne chère.

10. _____ verre dans lequel tu bois est en cristal de Baccarat.

Common gender hesitations made even by the French

It's always a good feeling not to be alone. Even the French are puzzled by the gender of certain words. When you run into a French person, test him or her on one of the words in the following lists. Masculine or feminine? Bet a **mousse au chocolat** or a bottle of champagne. You'll most likely win!

Feminine nouns

These feminine nouns are often wrongly used in the masculine by the French. You'll notice that many of these nouns start with a vowel or an **h**:

acné	_acne_	**écarlate**	_scarlet_	**oasis**	_oasis_
acoustique	_acoustics_	**échappatoire**	_way out_	**ocre**	_ochre_
aise	_ease_	**écharde**	_splinter_	**octave**	_octave_
alcôve	_alcove_	**écritoire**	_writing case_	**omoplate**	_shoulder blade_

alternance	*alternation*	**enclume**	*anvil*	**optique**	*optics*
amnistie	*amnesty*	**épice**	*spice*	**orbite**	*orbit*
anagramme	*anagram*	**épigramme**	*epigram*	**orge**	*barley*
ancre	*anchor*	**épithète**	*epithet*	**orthographe**	*spelling*
apostrophe	*apostrophe*	**équerre**	*set square*	**ouïe**	*hearing sense*
appendicite	*appendicitis*	**espèce**	*species*	**pulpe**	*pulp*
arabesque	*arabesque*	**hécatombe**	*slaughter*	**sépia**	*sepia*
argile	*clay*	**hélice**	*propeller*	**silicone**	*silicone*
armoire	*wardrobe*	**horloge**	*clock*	**stalactite**	*stalactite*
artère	*artery*	**idylle**	*idyll, romance*	**stalagmite**	*stalagmite*
atmosphère	*atmosphere*	**impasse**	*dead end*	**steppe**	*steppe*
autoroute	*highway*	**insulte**	*insult*	**ténèbres**	*darkness*
azalée	*azalea*	**météorite**	*meteorite*	**topaze**	*topaze*
câpre	*caper*	**molécule**	*molecule*	**urticaire**	*hives*
coriandre	*coriander*	**mousson**	*monsoon*	**vipère**	*viper*
dupe	*dupe*	**moustiquaire**	*mosquito net/screen*	**vis**	*screw*
ébène	*ebony*	**nacre**	*mother-of-pearl*	**volte-face**	*about-turn*

Léon a **l'ouïe fine**.
La noix de muscade est **l'épice parfaite** pour un soufflé au fromage.

*Léon has **sharp hearing**.*
*Nutmeg is **the perfect spice** for a cheese soufflé.*

Masculine nouns

The following masculine nouns are often incorrectly identified as feminine by the French:

abîme	*abyss, gulf*	**camée**	*cameo*	**haltère**	*dumbbell*
abysse	*abyss*	**camélia**	*camellia*	**hectare**	*hectare*
agrume	*citrus fruit*	**cèpe**	*porcini mushroom*	**hémisphère**	*hemisphere*
ail	*garlic*	**cerne**	*shadow (eyes)*	**incendie**	*fire/blaze*
air	*air*	**chrysanthème**	*chrysanthemum*	**indice**	*clue*
alcool	*alcohol*	**décombres**	*rubble*	**interstice**	*crack*
amber	*amber*	**éclair**	*lightning, éclair*	**intervalle**	*interval*
amiante	*asbestos*	**effluve**	*smell*	**ivoire**	*ivory*
anathème	*anathema*	**élastique**	*rubber band*	**jade**	*jade*
anchois	*anchovy*	**éloge**	*praise*	**leurre**	*delusion*
anniversaire	*birthday*	**emblème**	*emblem*	**losange**	*lozenge*
antidote	*antidote*	**en-tête**	*header, heading*	**média**	*media*
aparté	*aside*	**entracte**	*intermission*	**météore**	*meteor*
appétit	*appetite*	**épiderme**	*skin*	**myrte**	*myrtle*
armistice	*armistice*	**épilogue**	*epilogue*	**narcisse**	*narcissus*
aromate	*seasoning*	**épisode**	*episode*	**obélisque**	*obelisk*
arôme	*aroma*	**équilibre**	*balance*	**organe**	*organ*

arpège	*arpeggio*	**équinoxe**	*equinox*	**orteil**	*toe*
ascenseur	*elevator*	**escalier**	*staircase*	**ovale**	*oval*
astérisque	*asterisk*	**été**	*summer*	**poulpe**	*octopus*
atome	*atom*	**exode**	*exodus*	**tentacule**	*tentacle*
augure	*omen*	**girofle**	*clove*	**trèfle**	*clover*
automne	*autumn*	**globule**	*globule*	**tubercule**	*tubercle*
basalte	*basalt*	**glucose**	*glucose*	**ustensile**	*utensil*

Ils ont construit **un escalier** en colimaçon.
L'exode rural a eu un terrible impact sur cette région.

*They built **a spiral staircase**.*
***Rural exodus** had a terrible impact on this region.*

Gender changes over time

Once French replaced Latin in France, the neutral gender disappeared. Over time, some nouns changed gender. For instance, the following feminine nouns have become masculine:

caprice	*whim*	**honneur**	*honor*	**orage**	*thunderstorm*
comté	*county*	**horoscope**	*horoscope*	**poison**	*poison*
doute	*doubt*	**losange**	*lozenge*	**reproche**	*reproach*
duché	*dukedom*	**mélange**	*mix*	**silence**	*silence*
jour	*day*	**mensonge**	*lie*	**soupçon**	*suspicion*
exemple	*example*	**navire**	*ship*		

Dans la littérature du dix-neuvième siècle, **le poison préféré** était l'arsenic.
Encourager **le mensonge** est **un mauvais exemple** pour les jeunes.

*In nineteenth-century literature, **the favorite poison** was arsenic.*
*Encouraging **lying** is **a bad example** for children.*

And over time, the following nouns have become feminine:

affaire	*affair/business*	**ébène**	*ebony*	**image**	*image*
alarme	*alarm*	**épithète**	*epithet, attribute*	**marge**	*margin*
armoire	*wardrobe*	**épée**	*sword*	**offre**	*offer*
comète	*comet*	**erreur**	*error, mistake*	**ombre**	*shadow*
date	*date*	**estime**	*esteem*	**orthographe**	*spelling*
dent	*tooth*	**horloge**	*clock*		

Balzac écrivait beaucoup de notes dans **la marge** de ses livres.
Cette date vous convient?

*Balzac wrote many notes in **the margins** of his books.*
*Is **this date** convenient for you?*

Gender differences between France and Quebec

The following nouns, borrowed from other languages, are used in the masculine in France and in the feminine in Quebec:

bogue *(computer bug)*
business
gang
mozzarella

pina colada
rave
sandwich

Toute **la gang** était là pour célébrer l'anniversaire d'Ève.

La **business** que j'ai faite avec lui a très bien marché.

*The whole **gang** was there to celebrate Ève's birthday.*

The business I did with her worked very well.

EXERCICE

7·3

Traduire les phrases suivantes en utilisant *tu* si nécessaire.

1. The stain on your shirt is probably a wine stain.

_____

2. All the women wore red silk dresses at the ball.

_____

3. These workers' struggle will last a long time.

_____

4. You are lucky! They opened the way for you.

_____

5. The trunk you brought to Paris is too heavy.

_____

6. Mélanie wants to see the greenhouse.

_____

7. I don't know the tribe she described at the conference.

_____

8. The pair of shoes she bought is really beautiful.

   _____

9. My brother lost the tennis racket I gave him.

   _____

10. The last time you were here was in December.

    _____

Are we all done finally, you may wonder? Not really. On a regular basis, *Le Robert* and *Le Larousse* and other dictionaries add dozens of new words. Just as anthropologists observe mores, lexicographers observe the frequency of the usage of new words and decide if they deserve to be entered in the dictionary. Recently added, for example: **le smoothie**, **la saladerie**, **la cranberry**, and **le cheesecake**.

Indeed, there is hope, a lot of it—and, along with it, humor and laughter. Genders are funny in their disarming irrationality; savor that irrationality, revel in it, let it lead you to a state of euphoria that will facilitate the learning process. For example, there is something intrinsically funny about the fact (which grammarians may be able to explain) that the word **pape** (*pope*) used to be feminine in French. Also, think of Mark Twain and his brilliant satirical piece "The Awful German Language," particularly the section that lampoons German genders. When someone says, "Where did the young lady go?" a German answers, "It went to the opera." I'm sure Twain knew that there was nothing illogical in the fact that the German word *Mädchen*, being a diminutive, required the neuter gender, as do all diminutives in German. However, being a humorist, Twain chose to ignore the facts and focus on the ostensible absurdity of saying *it* in referring to a young woman. While I'm certainly not encouraging you to ignore grammatical explanations, I think that you will derive much pleasure from the apparent absurdity of certain linguistic phenomena. Twain could have written a similar spoof of any other language, especially French.

Above all, hang on! Review noun endings on a regular basis, and try to remember the exceptions. Incorporate words into stories, and you'll never forget that the word **le musée**, despite its -ée ending, is masculine, and **la voile** should not confused with **le voile**:

Et si on allait au **musée**, ou bien faire de **la voile**?	*What about going to the museum or sailing?*

You have reached an important point in your peregrinations through the wild world of genders. While at first your journey may have seemed arduous, I can assure you that it will be smooth sailing from now on.

Féminin, masculin forever

Comprehensive exercises

EXERCICE
8·1

Compléter avec l'article défini *le, la* ou *l'.*

1. _____ cadeau

2. _____ victime

3. _____ éventail

4. _____ firmament

5. _____ charade

6. _____ mirage

7. _____ bêtise

8. _____ espoir

9. _____ Pologne

10. _____ comparaison

11. _____ dictature

12. _____ pétition

13. _____ centaine

14. _____ vaccin

15. _____ leçon

16. _____ réveillon

17. _____ Crête

18. _____ mariage

19. _____ culture

20. _____ merveille

Compléter avec l'article défini *le, la* ou *l'*.

1. _____ ballet

2. _____ tristesse

3. _____ girafe

4. _____ fourmi

5. _____ perce-neige

6. _____ camélia

7. _____ violet

8. _____ lenteur

9. _____ météore

10. _____ tulipe

11. _____ lin

12. _____ parapluie

13. _____ cocotte minute

14. _____ amnistie

15. _____ chapeau

16. _____ hamac

17. _____ jardin

18. _____ frère

19. _____ nuit

20. _____ chocolat

Compléter avec l'article défini ou indéfini *un, une, le* ou *la* selon le sens.

1. Quand _____ printemps arrivera, _____ cerisier de notre jardin sera en fleur.

2. _____ groupe de touristes chinois se promène le long de _____ Seine.

3. _____ champagne qu'Angèle nous a offert est _____ meilleur.

4. _____ pull en mohair qu'elle tricote est pour _____ femme de Yan.

5. _____ Golf que mon frère a achetée est gris métallique.

6. Tu dois lui offrir une bague en citrine. _____ citrine est sa pierre favorite.

7. _____ TGV Lyon-Paris aura trente minutes de retard.

8. On a mal dormi car _____ matelas de l'hôtel était trop mou.

9. Peux-tu m'expliquer _____ pourquoi et _____ comment de cette situation?

10. _____ lave-vaisselle est en panne mais _____ restaurant vietnamien au coin de la rue est ouvert jusqu'à minuit.

Compléter en mettant la profession au féminin.

EXAMPLE   Lui, il est psychologue. Moi, je ne serai jamais psychologue! Je serai (consultant).

Lui, il est psychologue. Moi, je ne serai jamais psychologue! Je serai consultante.

1. Lui, il est dentiste. Moi... (traducteur)

_____

2. Lui il est PDG. Moi... (viticulteur)

_____

3. Lui, il est chanteur. Moi... (danseur)

_____

4. Lui, il est duc. Moi... (prince)

_____

5. Lui, il est technicien. Moi... (dessinateur)

_____

6. Lui, il est couturier. Moi... (mannequin)

_____

7. Lui, il est doyen. Moi... (pharmacien)

_____

8. Lui, il est avocat. Moi... (infirmier)

_____

9. Lui, il est coiffeur. Moi... (chocolatier)

_____

10. Lui, il est ouvrier. Moi... (commerçant)

_____

EXERCICE 8·5

Compléter avec l'article défini *le*, *la* ou *l'*.

1. Donne-moi _____ casse-noisette qui est sur _____ buffet.

2. _____ dessus de la table de jardin a été abîmé par _____ pluie.

3. Ferme _____ porte-fenêtre sinon il fera froid dans _____ salon.

4. Je dois rapporter _____ drap-housse. Ce n'est pas la bonne taille.

5. _____ invité de Victor a cassé _____ porte-savon en terre cuite du Maroc.

6. Sans _____ main-d'œuvre étrangère, _____ nourriture coûterait plus cher.

7. Tu veux _____ langue de chat ou _____ madeleine?

8. Élizabeth travaille dans _____ seul gratte-ciel de _____ ville.

9. Voici _____ clé du garage. Mets-la sur _____ porte-clés!

10. J'entends _____ rire de Carole dans _____ voiture-restaurant. Allons la rejoindre!

EXERCICE
8·6

Compléter avec l'article indéfini _un_, _une_ ou _des_.

1. Elle était sur _____ bateau à voile quand _____ vague l'a complètement arrosée.

2. Clément a acheté _____ vase en céramique pour _____ amie qui s'est occupée de son chat pendant son congé sabbatique.

3. Noé a perdu _____ somme considérable dans _____ casino de Trouville.

4. Voici _____ moule que Rodin a utilisé pour _____ de ses sculptures.

5. Donne-moi _____ poêle pour faire _____ crêpes.

6. Nous étions assis sur _____ banc en chêne et elle me chantait _____ ballade.

7. Mon beau-frère a pêché _____ carpe dans _____ lac près de notre chalet.

8. Avec _____ telle politique étrangère, ils courent au désastre.

9. À Sadec, dans la ville de Duras, le lit était recouvert de _____ moustiquaire.

10. Nous cherchons _____ gîte dans le Périgord pour _____ semaine.

Compléter le haïku de Bashô avec *le, la, l'* ou *les.*

Pleine lune.

J'ai tourné toute _____ nuit

autour de _____ étang...

Avec _____ cloison de papier blanc

_____ asphodèles blancs

échangent leur lumière.

Belles du matin.

Durant _____ jour, _____ porte est hermétiquement fermée:

clôture de _____ maison.

Brise légère.

_____ ombre de _____ glycine

Tremble à peine...

—Bashô (1644–1694)

Compléter le passage de *La Vénus d'Ille* avec l'article défini *le, la, l'* ou *les.*

_____ arrangements du lendemain furent réglés de _____ manière suivante. Tout

_____ monde devait être prêt et en toilette à dix heures précises. _____ chocolat

pris, on se rendrait en voiture à Puygarrig. _____ mariage civil devait se faire à _____ mairie du village, et _____ cérémonie religieuse dans _____ chapelle du château. Viendrait ensuite un déjeuner. Après _____ déjeuner on passerait _____ temps comme l'on pourrait jusqu'à sept heures. À sept heures, on retournerait à Ille, chez M. de Peyrehorade, où devaient souper _____ deux familles réunies. _____ reste s'ensuit naturellement. Ne pouvant danser, on avait voulu manger _____ plus possible.

Dès huit heures j'étais assis devant _____ Vénus, un crayon à _____ main, recommençant pour _____ vingtième fois la tête de _____ statue, sans pouvoir parvenir à en saisir _____ expression. M. de Peyrehorade allait et venait autour de moi, me donnait des conseils, me répétait ses étymologies phéniciennes puis disposait des roses du Bengale sur _____ piédestal de _____ statue, et d'un ton tragi-comique lui adressait des vœux pour _____ couple qui allait vivre sous son toit. Vers neuf heures il rentra pour songer à sa toilette, et en même temps parut M. Alphonse, bien serré dans un habit neuf, en gants blancs, souliers vernis, boutons ciselés, une rose à _____ boutonnière. [...]

Contre _____ attente générale, M. Alphonse manqua _____ première balle; il est vrai qu'elle vint rasant la terre et lancée avec une force surprenante par un Aragonais qui paraissait être _____ chef des Espagnols.

C'était un homme d'une quarantaine d'années, sec et nerveux, haut de six pieds, et sa peau olivâtre avait une teinte presque aussi foncée que _____ bronze de _____ Vénus.

M. Alphonse jeta sa raquette à terre avec fureur. « C'est cette maudite bague, s'écria-t-il, qui me serre _____ doigt, et me fait manquer une balle sûre! »

Il ôta, non sans peine, sa bague de diamants: je m'approchais pour la recevoir; mais il me prévint, courut à _____ Vénus, lui passa _____ bague au doigt annulaire, et reprit son poste à _____ tête des Illois. Il était pâle, mais calme et résolu. Dès lors il ne fit plus une seule faute, et _____ Espagnols furent battus complètement. Ce fut un beau spectacle que _____ enthousiasme des spectateurs: _____ uns poussaient mille cris de joie en jetant leurs bonnets en l'air; d'autres lui serraient les mains, l'appelant _____ honneur du pays. S'il eût repoussé une invasion, je doute qu'il eût reçu des félicitations plus vives et plus sincères. _____ chagrin des vaincus ajoutait encore à _____ éclat de sa victoire. [...]

« Vous avez bien mon anneau? poursuivit-il après un silence.

—Eh bien! on l'a pris?

—Non.

—En ce cas, vous l'avez?

—Non... je... Je ne puis l'ôter du doigt de cette diable de Vénus.

—Bon! vous n'avez pas tiré assez fort.

—Si fait... Mais _____ Vénus... elle a serré _____ doigt. »

—Prosper Mérimée, *La Vénus d'Ille* (1837)

Answer key

1 The magic and romance of French gender: Basic endings and other cases

1·1 1. la tolérance   2. le pain   3. le compliment   4. le sapin   5. la présence   6. le courage 7. l'agneau (*masc.*)   8. l'orangeraie (*fem.*)   9. la chaîne   10. la plage   11. le ruisseau 12. l'architecture (*fem.*)   13. le classement   14. le symbolisme   15. l'égalité (*fem.*) 16. l'odeur (*fem.*)   17. la pudeur   18. le vignoble   19. la paille   20. le calepin

1·2
J'aime l'eau
J'aime l'eau dans ma baignoire
Et sur le carrelage de la cuisine quand maman le nettoie
J'aime l'eau sur la plage
J'aime les vaguelettes
Qui me chatouillent les doigts de pieds
Et s'en vont avec la marée
J'aime l'eau des flaques et des étangs
Des lacs et des barrages où elle se heurte en écumant
J'aime la pluie qui me mouille la langue
Et qui fait pousser les plantes dans le jardin
J'aime l'eau des fleuves
L'eau où pullulent les petits poissons
J'aime l'eau quand elle est bien chaude
Le matin dans mon lavabo
J'aime l'eau quand elle est gelée
Quand je peux patiner sur les mares glacées.

1·3 1. le meuble   2. le soja   3. la référence   4. le cocktail   5. le rail   6. la fin 7. l'attitude (*fem.*)   8. le lainage   9. le parlement   10. la centaine   11. la sculpture 12. le libéralisme   13. le signal   14. la délicatesse   15. l'horlogerie (*fem.*)   16. le citadin 17. le tact   18. l'orthographe (*fem.*)   19. le clavecin   20. la fraternité

1·4 1. l'acacia (*masc.*)   2. la chanson   3. le portefeuille   4. le domino   5. la signature 6. l'écaille (*fem.*)   7. le millefeuille   8. le cinéma   9. la tribu   10. le tracteur 11. l'établissement (*masc.*)   12. l'altitude (*fem.*)   13. le hamac   14. le ghetto 15. la confirmation   16. la noix   17. la main   18. l'inclinaison (*fem.*)   19. la soif 20. la faim

2 What are you doing? Naming people and animals

2·1
1. Il est directeur. Elle est directrice.
2. Il est chanteur. Elle est chanteuse.
3. Il est gardien. Elle est gardienne.
4. Il est commerçant. Elle est commerçante.
5. Il est pédiatre. Elle est pédiatre.
6. Il est consultant. Elle est consultante.
7. Il est traducteur. Elle est traductrice.
8. Il est agriculteur. Elle est agricultrice.
9. Il est technicien. Elle est technicienne.
10. Il est psychologue. Elle est psychologue.
11. Il est assistant technique. Elle est assistante technique.
12. Il est astrologue. Elle est astrologue.
13. Il est mécanicien. Elle est mécanicienne.
14. Il est boucher. Elle est bouchère.
15. Il est électricien. Elle est électricienne.
16. Il est archiduc. Elle est archiduchesse.
17. Il est dessinateur. Elle est dessinatrice.
18. Il est baron. Elle est baronne.
19. Il est infirmier. Elle est infirmière.
20. Il est viticulteur. Elle est viticultrice.

2·2
1. Son cousin est une célébrité dans le monde du spectacle.
2. Une altesse royale que nous n'avons pas vraiment reconnue, a fait halte dans notre village hier.
3. Ta tante est un ange!
4. Mathieu est une personne sur qui on peut compter.
5. Sandrine est un mannequin célèbre pour ses coiffures excentriques.
6. Monsieur Thibault est un génie en informatique.
7. Sa femme est un gourmet par excellence.
8. Ce chanteur, c'est une idole depuis des années.
9. Ce type, c'est une véritable crapule!
10. Julie est un témoin que le juge veut entendre.

2·3
1. L'impresario et sa star prenaient un verre sur la Croisette.
2. Mélanie voudrait inviter son oncle et sa tante pour son anniversaire.
3. La police n'a pas encore retrouvé son assassin.
4. Hervé est arrivé avec Anna, son successeur.
5. Alice, tu es son sauveur!
6. Son parrain lui a offert un joli bracelet.
7. Lui et son acolyte, ils ne font que des bêtises!
8. Yan est venu nous voir avec son beau-frère et sa belle-mère.
9. Ce pays ne peut pas se débarrasser de son tyran.
10. Quelle est sa vedette préférée?

2·4 1. La nourrice de Félix est irlandaise.
2. Marc et le confrère de Vincent assisteront au colloque.
3. Au vernissage se trouvaient Picasso avec la muse d'Aragon.
4. C'est l'escroc que j'ai vu dans le journal!
5. La cantatrice que vous rencontrerez ce soir interprètera Aïda à l'Opéra Bastille en mars.
6. Avez-vous vu le valet?
7. Le vandale, tout vêtu de noir, a commencé à briser les vitres des voitures.
8. Le moine à l'entrée du monastère sera notre guide.
9. Comment s'appelle le baryton qui chantera Madame Butterfly?
10. La Bigoudène vend des galettes au marché de Quimper.

2·5 1. La vache est agacée par la mouche qui tourne autour de sa tête.
2. En théorie, le lièvre court plus vite que la tortue.
3. Le perroquet de la tante de Xavier répète sans cesse les mêmes mots.
4. Je veux choisir le chameau qui me plaît pour faire un tour dans le désert.
5. La louve et l'ourse protègent farouchement leurs petits.
6. La cigale chante pendant que la fourmi travaille.
7. LÉO, le chat de Mademoiselle Gallatin est un magnifique Maine Coon.
8. L'oiseau qui se perche sur notre balcon est un rouge-gorge.
9. As-tu mangé le saumon que tu as attrapé?
10. La guêpe qui était sur la table a fini par la piquer.

2·6 1. la chamelle/le chameau   2. la chèvre/le bouc   3. la truie/le porc   4. la louve/le loup
5. l'oie/le jars   6. la chevrette/le chevreuil   7. la jument/le cheval   8. l'agnelle/l'agneau
9. la biche/le cerf   10. la brebis/le bélier

3   Across the universe: Places and the calendar

3·1 1. la Californie   2. la Seine-Saint-Denis   3. la Louisiane   4. la Bretagne   5. la
Guadeloupe   6. le Caire   7. le Languedoc   8. la Dordogne   9. le Nebraska   10. le
Vermont   11. le Maine   12. la Lorraine   13. le New Jersey   14. le Limousin   15. le
Gard   16. le Poitou   17. le Missouri   18. la Provence   19. la Martinique   20. les
Alpes-Maritimes

3·2 1. la France   2. le Danemark   3. la Grèce   4. le Mexique   5. la Belgique   6. le Japon
7. le Chili   8. le Guatemala   9. le Brésil   10. le Cambodge   11. l'Italie   12. le
Portugal   13. la Chine   14. la Turquie   15. la Russie   16. la Bolivie   7. la Malaisie
18. la Nouvelle-Calédonie   19. le Costa Rica   20. les Philippines

3·3 1. Le Népal est un endroit idéal pour le trekking.
2. La Jordanie abrite l'ancienne cité de Pétra, patrimoine mondial de l'UNESCO.
3. En mars, Erwan visitera le Togo, le Bénin et la Sierra Leone.
4. La Nouvelle-Zélande attire Carla depuis longtemps.
5. La Guyane est un département ultramarin.
6. Le Burkina Faso organise un gigantesque festival de cinéma tous les deux ans.
7. Le Qatar a invité des architectes français pour construire des édifices.
8. Le Viêt-Nam a fortement influencé l'écriture de Marguerite Duras.
9. Les Pays-Bas sont de grands exportateurs de tulipes.
10. Le Québec est traversé par le Saint-Laurent.

3·4   1. le Rio Grande   2. la Somme   3. le Mékong   4. la Volga   5. la Loire   6. le
Mississippi   7. le Têt   8. le Drâ   9. le Niger   10. la Rance   11. le Potomac   12. le
Tumen   13. le Loir   14. la Seine   15. le Pô   16. la Drôme   17. le Nil   18. le Rhône
19. la Dordogne   20. la Vienne

3·5   L'automne (*masc.*) prochain, j'irai à l'Île Maurice dans l'océan (*masc.*) Indien. L'Île Maurice est
merveilleuse car c'est une île volcanique. Puis l'été (*masc.*) suivant, mon amie Anne et moi
envisageons de faire une croisière en Norvège. Anne connaît la mer Noire et le golfe du Mexique.
En raison du travail de ses parents, elle a beaucoup voyagé. Elle rêve de voir l'océan (*masc.*)
Pacifique. Nous irons sans doute ensemble un de ces jours.

4   Strawberry fields forever: Plants, wine, and cheese

4·1   1. Dans le jardin de Victoire, il y a un lilas et un laurier rose.
2. La rose sur ton chapeau est fanée.
3. Nous étions à la campagne et il a cueilli un bouton d'or.
4. Quand il était jeune, Bernard est tombé sur un cactus.
5. Le chrysanthème est l'emblème national du Japon.
6. La mariée tenait une orchidée de la main gauche.
7. Le séquoia que j'ai pris en photo faisait huit mètres de diamètre.
8. L'automobiliste s'est écrasé contre un platane.
9. Sur chaque table du restaurant, il y avait une rose rouge dans un vase noir.
10. Le chêne dans le jardin de mon grand-père a près de 150 ans.

4·2   1. La pivoine rose signifie la sincérité. Vous pouvez compter sur moi.
2. Le tournesol signifie que vous êtes mon soleil; je ne vois que vous.
3. La pensée signifie que je ne veux pas que vous m'oubliiez.
4. Le mimosa signifie que je doute de votre amour.
5. La jacinthe signifie que je suis conscient de votre beauté.
6. Le bégonia signifie que mon amitié pour vous est sincère.
7. La véronique signifie fidélité, âme sœur.
8. Le bouton d'or signifie que vous vous moquez de moi.
9. Le narcisse signifie l'égoïsme.
10. La rue signifie que j'aime l'indépendance.

4·3   Lucie a mis au milieu un demi-kiwi, puis un abricot, une petite poire. Ensuite, en forme de
bouquet, une mirabelle, un cassis, une cerise, une myrtille, une framboise, un cassis. À chaque
coin, elle a placé un marron et une cacahouète. Pour finir, elle a mis une truffe au chocolat pour
chaque invité tout autour du gâteau.

4·4   —Alex, qu'est-ce que tu prends? Un médoc et un beaufort?
—Non, aujourd'hui, je voudrais un rosé d'Anjou et un gorgonzola.
—Et toi, Yves?
—Une vodka et un vacherin.
—Une vodka? En quel honneur? Tu prends toujours un saumur!
—Oui mais demain, on part pour Moscou. Je veux m'habituer.
—D'accord, une vodka pour Yves et un chablis pour Raoul?

—Exact. Un chablis et un crottin de Chavignol.
—Tout le monde est servi?
—Non, Julien, tu m'as oublié. Un pernod et un chabichou.
—Désolé. Ça arrive tout de suite.

5 Like a rolling stone: Colors and fabric, the elements, cars, and brands and acronyms

5·1
1. Une poupée portait une robe en satin rose. L'autre portait une jupe en mousseline.
2. La future mariée veut porter une robe en organdi ivoire.
3. Sa fille aime les polaires blanches.
4. J'aimerais lui offrir une écharpe en cachemire rouge.
5. J'aime mes nouveaux gants bleus en Gore-Tex.
6. Ton pull en angora est si chaud.
7. La première dame porte souvent une longue robe en soie.
8. Le cuir de votre manteau est de grande qualité.
9. Son T-shirt en lycra est indigo.
10. Il porte toujours des costumes prince de Galles.

5·2
1. l'émeraude (*fem.*)   2. le diamant   3. la tourmaline   4. l'étain (*masc.*)
5. le potassium   6. le fer   7. le lithium   8. le marbre   9. la chaux   10. le charbon
11. la citrine   12. le quartz   13. la topaze   14. le bronze   15. le corail   16. le plomb
17. la bauxite   18. le sel   19. le jade   20. le rubis

5·3
Le père de mon copain Luc adore sa BMW alors que sa femme préfère sa Mini. Luc voudrait bien avoir son Pajero à lui tout seul mais ses parents ne sont pas d'accord. S'il passe le bac, il pourra rendre ses copains jaloux avec sa Smart ou sa Coccinelle.

5·4
1. Passe-moi le sel!
2. Le chef écrit toujours son menu sur une ardoise.
3. J'ai acheté des colliers en corail et en lapis lazuli en Inde.
4. Sa Volvo est grise et sa Clio est jaune citron.
5. Le festival de la BD a lieu chaque année à Angoulême.
6. Allons à la plage! L'iode est bon pour la santé.
7. Ce vase est en étain.
8. Si le vrai safran n'était pas si cher, je l'utiliserais chaque jour.
9. Ma voisine Louise a vu un OVNI hier soir dans le champ de maïs.
10. Ce TGV s'arrête-t-il à Amiens?

6 Speak to me: Other languages, parts of speech, and the sciences

6·1
1. Antoine apprend le japonais car il veut aussi apprendre le karaté.
2. Le marketing pour la vodka Van Gogh a bien réussi.
3. Le tweet a été envoyé par un gourou de l'ashram d'Aurobindo.
4. La pizza et la polenta qu'elle a préparées étaient délicieuses.

5. Je cherche un interprète qui parle très bien le chinois et le russe.
6. Le Carnaval de Venise a lieu en février.
7. Dans la datcha, cela sentait le bortsch et la vodka.
8. Akiko, aimez-vous le saké? Et le karaoké?
9. Le nouveau manga de Yoshihiro Togashi connaît un grand succès.
10. Ils ont chevauché dans la steppe de Mongolie.

6·2
1. Le nouvel abat-jour que tu as acheté est trop grand.
2. Le devant de la maison a besoin de réparations.
3. Je ne peux pas trouver le casse-noisette. Où l'as-tu mis?
4. Thierry lui a offert le presse-papier en cristal dont elle rêvait.
5. Clara se demandait le pourquoi de toute chose.
6. Ils envisagent de construire le plus haut gratte-ciel du monde.
7. Quentin étudie la philosophie et le droit à la Sorbonne.
8. À quelle heure ouvre la voiture-restaurant?
9. Le sous-marin *Le Redoutable* a fait une escale à Hawaï.
10. Le lave-vaisselle est en panne. Allons au restaurant!

6·3
1. L'arc-en-ciel était rouge, jaune, rose et bleu.
2. Leur fille étudie l'informatique à Paris.
3. Avez-vous vu la garde-robe de Sophie?
4. La sous-traitance est un phénomène de plus en plus commun.
5. Vous parlez espagnol ou italien?
6. Ce pays a une main-d'œuvre étrangère importante.
7. Le ginseng est bon pour la santé.
8. L'art qu'elle vend est très cher.
9. Laurent est célèbre pour son rire contagieux.
10. Des architectes français construiront ce nouveau gratte-ciel.

7 Anything goes: Other situations to keep in mind

7·1
1. Le livre qu'Éric a écrit est sur la mode en Italie.
2. Il a marché dans la vase et ses chaussures sont sales.
3. Le seul légume que mon fils accepte de manger, c'est le broccoli chinois.
4. Elles m'ont suggéré le gîte dans le Lot où elles ont séjourné l'an passé.
5. La crêpe a collé à la poêle. Elle est immangeable!
6. Tu savais que Jean s'était laissé pousser la barbe?
7. Voudrais-tu faire de la voile au large de l'Île de Ré?
8. On doit lire le roman jusqu'à la page 150?
9. Xavier a oublié le mémoire qu'il doit remettre à son professeur.
10. La mousse pour le bain est parfumée à la lavande.

7·2
1. Je n'ai pas pu enlever la tache de vin sur ta chemise.
2. Le maître-nageur a mis le drapeau rouge car la mer est très agitée.
3. La diva a perdu la voix au beau milieu de l'aria.
4. Vous aurez la peau lisse si vous utilisez cette crème hydratante.
5. La police a trouvé le repaire des trafiquants de drogue.
6. Attention! La sole jaune est tombée sur le sol.
7. Je ne connais pas la tribu dont elle a parlé lors de sa conférence.

8. Lucie a vu le plus vieux chêne de sa vie dans la forêt de Tronçais.
9. Prépare un bon repas. Bertrand aime la bonne chère.
10. Le verre dans lequel tu bois est en cristal de Baccarat.

7·3
1. La tache sur ta chemise est sans doute une tache de vin.
2. Toutes les femmes portaient des robes en soie rouge au bal.
3. La lutte de ces ouvriers durera longtemps.
4. Tu as de la chance! Ils ont ouvert la voie pour toi.
5. La malle que tu as apportée à Paris est trop lourde.
6. Mélanie veut voir la serre.
7. Je ne connais pas la tribu qu'elle a décrite à la conférence.
8. La paire de chaussures qu'elle a achetée est vraiment belle.
9. Mon frère a perdu la raquette de tennis que je lui ai donnée.
10. La dernière fois que tu étais ici, c'était en décembre.

8   Féminin, masculin forever: Comprehensive exercises

8·1
1. le cadeau   2. la victime   3. l'éventail   4. le firmament   5. la charade   6. le mirage
7. la bêtise   8. l'espoir   9. la Pologne   10. la comparaison   11. la dictature   12. la
pétition   13. la centaine   14. le vaccin   15. la leçon   16. le réveillon   17. la Crête
18. le mariage   19. la culture   20. la merveille

8·2
1. le ballet   2. la tristesse   3. la girafe   4. la fourmi   5. le/la perce-neige   6. le
camélia   7. le violet   8. la lenteur   9. le météore   10. la tulipe   11. le lin   12. le
parapluie   13. la cocotte minute   14. l'amnistie   15. le chapeau   16. le hamac   17. le
jardin   18. le frère   19. la nuit   20. le chocolat

8·3
1. Quand le printemps arrivera, le cerisier de notre jardin sera en fleur.
2. Le groupe de touristes chinois se promène le long de la Seine.
3. Le champagne qu'Angèle nous a offert est le meilleur.
4. Le pull en mohair qu'elle tricote est pour la femme de Yan.
5. La Golf que mon frère a achetée est gris métallique.
6. Tu dois lui offrir une bague en citrine. La citrine est sa pierre favorite.
7. Le TGV Lyon-Paris aura trente minutes de retard.
8. On a mal dormi car le matelas de l'hôtel était trop mou.
9. Peux-tu m'expliquer le pourquoi et le comment de cette situation?
10. Le lave-vaisselle est en panne mais le restaurant vietnamien au coin de la rue est ouvert
jusqu'à minuit.

8·4
1. Lui, il est dentiste. Moi, je ne serai jamais dentiste! Je serai traductrice.
2. Lui, il est PDG. Moi, je ne serai jamais PDG! Je serai viticultrice.
3. Lui, il est chanteur. Moi, je ne serai jamais chanteuse! Je serai danseuse.
4. Lui, il est duc. Moi, je ne serai jamais duchesse! Je serai princesse.
5. Lui, il est technicien. Moi, je ne serai jamais technicienne! Je serai dessinatrice.
6. Lui, il est couturier. Moi, je ne serai jamais couturier! Je serai mannequin.
7. Lui, il est doyen. Moi, je ne serai jamais doyenne! Je serai pharmaciennne.
8. Lui, il est avocat. Moi, je ne serai jamais avocate! Je serai infirmière.
9. Lui, il est coiffeur. Moi, je ne serai jamais coiffeuse! Je serai chocolatière.
10. Lui, il est ouvrier. Moi, je ne serai jamais ouvrière! Je serai commerçante.

8·5
1. Donne-moi le casse-noisette qui est sur le buffet.
2. Le dessus de la table de jardin a été abîmé par la pluie.
3. Ferme la porte-fenêtre sinon il fera froid dans le salon.
4. Je dois rapporter le drap-housse. Ce n'est pas la bonne taille.
5. L'invité de Victor a cassé le porte-savon en terre cuite du Maroc.
6. Sans la main-d'œuvre étrangère, la nourriture coûterait plus cher.
7. Tu veux la langue de chat ou la madeleine?
8. Élizabeth travaille dans le seul gratte-ciel de la ville.
9. Voici la clé du garage. Mets-la sur le porte-clés!
10. J'entends le rire de Carole dans la voiture-restaurant. Allons la rejoindre!

8·6
1. Elle était sur un bateau à voile quand une vague l'a complètement arrosée.
2. Clément a acheté un vase en céramique pour une amie qui s'est occupée de son chat pendant son congé sabbatique.
3. Noé a perdu une somme considérable dans un casino de Trouville.
4. Voici un moule que Rodin a utilisé pour une de ses sculptures.
5. Donne-moi une poêle pour faire des crêpes.
6. Nous étions assis sur un banc en chêne et elle me chantait une ballade.
7. Mon beau-frère a pêché une carpe dans un lac près de notre chalet.
8. Avec une telle politique étrangère, ils courent au désastre.
9. À Sadec, dans la ville de Duras, le lit était recouvert d'une moustiquaire.
10. Nous cherchons un gîte dans le Périgord pour une semaine.

8·7
Pleine lune.

J'ai tourné toute la nuit

autour de l'étang...

Avec la cloison de papier blanc

les asphodèles blancs

échangent leur lumière.

Belles du matin.

Durant le jour, la porte est hermétiquement fermée:

clôture de la maison.

Brise légère.

L'ombre de la glycine

Tremble à peine...

8·8
Les arrangements du lendemain furent réglés de la manière suivante. Tout le monde devait être prêt et en toilette à dix heures précises. Le chocolat pris, on se rendrait en voiture à Puygarrig. Le mariage civil devait se faire à la mairie du village, et la cérémonie religieuse dans la chapelle du château. Viendrait ensuite un déjeuner. Après le déjeuner on passerait le temps comme l'on pourrait jusqu'à sept heures. À sept heures, on retournerait à Ille, chez M. de Peyrehorade, où devaient souper les deux familles réunies. Le reste s'ensuit naturellement. Ne pouvant danser, on avait voulu manger le plus possible.

Dès huit heures j'étais assis devant la Vénus, un crayon à la main, recommençant pour la vingtième fois la tête de la statue, sans pouvoir parvenir à en saisir l'expression. M. de Peyrehorade allait et venait autour de moi, me donnait des conseils, me répétait ses étymologies phéniciennes puis disposait des roses du Bengale sur le piédestal de la statue, et d'un ton tragi-comique lui adressait des vœux pour le couple qui allait vivre sous son toit. Vers neuf heures il rentra pour songer à sa toilette, et en même temps parut M. Alphonse, bien serré dans un habit neuf, en gants blancs, souliers vernis, boutons ciselés, une rose à la boutonnière. [...]

Contre l'attente générale, M. Alphonse manqua la première balle; il est vrai qu'elle vint rasant la terre et lancée avec une force surprenante par un Aragonais qui paraissait être le chef des Espagnols.

C'était un homme d'une quarantaine d'années, sec et nerveux, haut de six pieds, et sa peau olivâtre avait une teinte presque aussi foncée que le bronze de la Vénus.

M. Alphonse jeta sa raquette à terre avec fureur. « C'est cette maudite bague, s'écria-t-il, qui me serre le doigt, et me fait manquer une balle sûre! »

Il ôta, non sans peine, sa bague de diamants: je m'approchais pour la recevoir; mais il me prévint, courut à la Vénus, lui passa la bague au doigt annulaire, et reprit son poste à la tête des Illois. Il était pâle, mais calme et résolu. Dès lors il ne fit plus une seule faute, et les Espagnols furent battus complètement. Ce fut un beau spectacle que l'enthousiasme des spectateurs: les uns poussaient mille cris de joie en jetant leurs bonnets en l'air; d'autres lui serraient les mains, l'appelant l'honneur du pays. S'il eût repoussé une invasion, je doute qu'il eût reçu des félicitations plus vives et plus sincères. Le chagrin des vaincus ajoutait encore à l'éclat de sa victoire. [...]

« Vous avez bien mon anneau? poursuivit-il après un silence.

—Eh bien! on l'a pris?

—Non.

—En ce cas, vous l'avez?

—Non... je... Je ne puis l'ôter du doigt de cette diable de Vénus.

—Bon! vous n'avez pas tiré assez fort.

—Si fait... Mais la Vénus... elle a serré le doigt. »

Index